PRAISE FOR JOYCE CHOPRA

"Joyce Chopra, what a gift of an extraordinary filmmaker you are, and one of our great pioneers who forged a very difficult path. And for female filmmakers everywhere, we are so blessed to have you as a storyteller to forge the way to make it easier for others."

—Laura Dern, actor

"Joyce Chopra has written a devastatingly frank, candid, and unsparing memoir of her life as a film director—a 'woman director' in a field notoriously dominated by men. The reader is astonished on her behalf, at times infuriated, moved to laughter, and then to tears. *Lady Director: Adventures in Hollywood, Television, and Beyond* is one of its kind—highly recommended."

—Joyce Carol Oates, author of
"Where Are You Going, Where Have You Been?"

"Joyce Chopra paved the way for future female filmmakers, and this book illuminates how ahead of her time she has always been. Her honesty is refreshing as she lets readers into her life, detailing her relationships, friendships, personal triumphs and devastating tragedies. Here is a woman who has nothing to lose, who is ready to tell her story, from her perspective, in her own words, with no holding back. I only wish I'd had this book to read when I was a shy teenage girl, to give me extra confidence as I dreamed of my own career in film."

—Alicia Malone, TCM host and author of *Girls on Film:
Lessons From a Life of Watching Women in Movies*

"Joyce Chopra's memoir is like a mentor in my pocket. Her vibrant writing makes me feel like I'm right there next to her, and her stories resonate with me and inspire me as a filmmaker and artist working today."

—Alexi Pappas, filmmaker and author of
Bravey: Chasing Dreams, Befriending Pain, and Other Big Ideas

"*Lady Director* is not just a fascinating memoir, but an entertaining, inspiring and occasionally outrage-inducing report from the frontlines of filmmaking. An absolute must-read for anyone interested in the history of American cinema."

—Elizabeth Weitzman, film critic and author of
Renegade Women in Film & TV

"Through the lens of an extraordinary, determined and adventurous career, *Lady Director* reminds us that present-day female Oscar nominees for Best Director stand on the shoulders of women like Joyce Chopra. This surprising, often shocking book is destined to become a classic."

—Honor Moore, author of *Our Revolution:*
A Mother and Daughter at Midcentury

"Chopra's memoir—both personal and political—is a deeply necessary corrective to histories of cinema and tales of the great artists of the '60s and '70s that tend to focus on big men and their big movies. Like all of Chopra's work, this memoir candidly reminds us of the injustices that structure our world, and gently says, we can do better. The book is a gift to all of us digging for authentic, revealing stories about the lives of women artists."

—Shilyh Warren, author of *Subject to Reality:*
Women and Documentary

"*Lady Director* is a bold, sometimes devastating, uncommonly honest and brilliant story of the inextricable nature of art and life, where few have feared to tread in cinema or on the page. Having already blessed film culture with at least two all-time masterpieces (*Joyce at 34* and *Smooth Talk*), Joyce Chopra's crucial memoir may be her most lasting contribution. A rare and great work that will be read for years to come, and that we are lucky to have."

—Jacob Perlin, Founding Artistic Director of Metrograph,
and distributor, "The Film Desk"

LADY DIRECTOR

LADY DIRECTOR

Adventures in Hollywood, Television and Beyond

JOYCE CHOPRA

CITY LIGHTS | SAN FRANCISCO

ISBN: 978-0-87286-868-7
eISBN: 978-0-87286-869-4

Library of Congress Cataloging-in-Publication Data

Names: Chopra, Joyce, author.
Title: Lady director : adventures in Hollywood, television and beyond /
Joyce Chopra.
Description: San Francisco : City Lights, [2022]
Identifiers: LCCN 2022014882 | ISBN 9780872868687 (paperback) | ISBN
9780872868694 (ebook)
Subjects: LCSH: Chopra, Joyce. | Women motion picture producers and
directors—United States—Biography. | Women television producers and
directors—United States—Biography. | Motion picture
industry—California—Los Angeles—History. | Television
broadcasting—California—Los Angeles—History. | LCGFT:
Autobiographies.
Classification: LCC PN1998.3.C64575 A3 2022 | DDC 791.4302/33092
[B]—dc23/eng/20220713
LC record available at https://lccn.loc.gov/2022014882

City Lights Books are published at the City Lights Bookstore
261 Columbus Avenue, San Francisco, CA 94133
citylights.com

contents

PROLOGUE ....*xiii*

CHAPTER ONE *1*

CHAPTER TWO *11*

CHAPTER THREE *23*

CHAPTER FOUR *39*

CHAPTER FIVE *51*

CHAPTER SIX *61*

CHAPTER SEVEN *75*

CHAPTER EIGHT *87*

CHAPTER NINE *119*

CHAPTER TEN *129*

CHAPTER ELEVEN *141*

CHAPTER TWELVE *151*

CHAPTER THIRTEEN *165*

CHAPTER FOURTEEN...*175*

CHAPTER FIFTEEN *187*

CHAPTER SIXTEEN *201*

POSTSCRIPT *213*

LADY DIRECTOR

prologue

W HEN I WAS about twenty-two or so, I purchased a Bolex film
camera and never once dared to use it. It just sat on a tripod
in the corner of my room, staring at me reproachfully. Becoming a
movie director had taken a firm grip on my imagination, but I hadn't
the vaguest idea of how one managed to do that. There weren't any
film schools that I knew of, and, even more problematic, I couldn't
picture myself in the director's role since I had never seen a movie
directed by a woman. Even the film history books that I collected to
educate myself never mentioned a single one. It didn't strike me as
odd; it was 1958, and that was the way the world was.

I would have been astonished if anyone had told me that a
French woman exactly my age, Alice Guy, was the first person to
direct a one-minute movie with actors in 1896 in Paris, or that
twenty years later, an American woman, Lois Weber, would become
the first person to direct a feature-length film, an adaptation of
The Merchant of Venice, for the newly formed Universal Studios
in Hollywood. I would have been equally amazed to be told that
another woman I never heard of, Dorothy Arzner, directed major
films all through the 1930s starring the likes of Katharine Hepburn
and Joan Crawford, having begun her own transition into the new
world of "talkies" along with the silent movie star Clara Bow. Miss
Bow's fear of microphones was so intense that it prompted Arzner
to invent the boom mike by attaching a microphone to a fishing
pole that followed the actress around the set where she couldn't
see it.

But none of these accomplishments would be recognized until
many years later when scholars began to uncover women's roles in

the early days of moviemaking. It's frustrating to think that I knew nothing of their work at a time when it would have helped me to feel less insane to think of such a career for myself. But even if I had known that other women had once been successful film directors, I would have been dismayed that their success didn't last. By the 1940s, when Hollywood became a very corporate world, not one woman could be found sitting in the director's chair except for the actress Ida Lupino, who survived by forming her own production company and hiring herself.

Like Lupino, I too had started my own business — Club 47, a folk music venue in Harvard Square — that drew a devoted audience from the day it opened. But once the club was up and running, I became restless and unable to stop myself from obsessing about making movies. I even started a weekly film series on the nights we were closed so I could see films I had only read about, and then watched them a second time to take notes on how they were shot. In a way these private viewings were harmful; the more I learned, the more convinced I became that I was deluding myself. How could I possibly think I could be part of such magic? I also doubted that I had the courage to leave my familiar world behind to venture into the great unknown. It took a year, but obsession finally won out. I gave my treasured Bolex to a friend who I hoped would actually use it and sold my share in the club to my partner Paula. With fifteen hundred dollars in my wallet and a backpack, I set out to find my way.

I wish I could say that I found that yellow brick road that magically led to my longed-for destination. When asked, especially by young women, how I finally managed to make numerous documentaries and feature films in spite of the often hostile road I had to travel on, I've never been able to give a useful reply. I am hoping that by writing about my adventures and summoning up the variety of people I met along the way—great actors like the irresistible Laura Dern or Diane Keaton, both of whom I directed, or the notable producer/director Sydney Pollack, who had me fired from a major studio feature—I will offer up some answers. It's also my hope that I'll learn some things about myself as I write, things I've never taken the time to question. As for children, husbands and lovers, they too are here since a life's work story would be even less complete without them. And, of course, close family, since that's where it all began.

one

M Y FATHER WAS taking such long steps down Mermaid Avenue that I had a hard time keeping up with him. We were on our way to visit a client of his — Izzy Einhorn — who owned a typewriter store, probably the only one in Coney Island. The two men paid no attention to me as I strolled the cramped aisles and pretended to type. Pretend because I was too small to press down hard enough on the big round keys and strike the black ribbon.

My father had the bad luck to earn his law degree during the early 1930s, at the bottom of the Great Depression, so he set up shop in his hometown, Coney Island, with small-time carnival ride owners as his first paying clients. To me they seemed like giants as I looked up at them in their booths, fingering rolls of paper tickets with their enormous hands. Down the alleyway, Mazie Gordon, the gravelly voiced Queen of the Bowery, presided majestically over her bump-em scooter ride, her floppy hat astride the silvered metal curlers in her bleached blonde hair and a lit cigarette dangling from her ruby lips. When she saw me, she would wave me a smile, and I was dying to ask her if it was true she patrolled the aisles of her movie theater in some faraway place called Manhattan and whacked the sleeping drunks with rolled-up newspapers if they snored through more than two showings of cartoons and double features. But I didn't dare put my special status in jeopardy by speaking up. Being "Kalina's Kid" meant free rides, and I could command a scooter for a whole afternoon if I wished, crashing into the metal cars of the other kids at high speed but never brave enough to attempt the Parachute Jump on the Boardwalk.

Yet the streets and alleys of Coney weren't always a source of delight. The World in Wax Musee with its photos of two-headed babies, a limbless woman, and a five-year-old mother from Peru named Lina scared the wits out of me, as I was exactly Lina's age. The worst was under the boardwalk where it was all shadow and danger, with men fumbling with something inside their trousers and grinning at me as I ran by as fast as I could, trying to catch up with my mother and older brother David as they dragged folding chairs, egg-salad sandwiches and soda onto the beach. The sand was so jammed with sprawling bodies to step over, we felt ourselves lucky just to find a few square feet to call our very own.

Coney Island was my father's home turf where he and his seven siblings were raised, he being next to youngest. That privilege belonged to my handsome Uncle Jack, and the two were always in competition. Their parents had emigrated from Russia and opened a boardinghouse, Kalina's Baths, with its back gate leading out to the beach. Every summer, when school was out, the kids had to handle the lockers bathers rented by the day, then clean the rooms of the weekly boarders. That's how my parents, Abe and Tillie, met when they were kids. During the summer, while her father worked as a tailor in a clothing factory over in Manhattan — his specialty, collars and sleeves — he deposited his wife and children at the beach to escape the heat, coming out on the weekends to be with them for he also loved to swim.

My father's father, Isaac Kalina, took a different path. Young Isaac met his future wife Rebecca at her father's house somewhere outside Odessa, the family prosperous enough to take in a Talmudic scholar. I was never told how the young couple came to live in Brooklyn at the turn of the twentieth century, and I was too young and foolish to ask. It's possible that Isaac was about to be drafted into the Russian Army and decided it was time to escape. It was said that his bride missed her family so much, or the comforts of her old life, that she crossed the ocean three times to be with her parents, taking her children with her. One or two were even born there. Since travelling in steerage was a famously miserable affair, I never quite believed in these tales until my cousin Richard (handsome Uncle Jack's son) discovered a manifest from the SS *Columbia* that lists our grandmother's final arrival at Ellis Island in 1906 with four of their kids. Since her husband had no skills outside debating the finer points of the Talmud, Rebecca, like so many other uprooted women, turned her homemaking skills into supporting her ever-growing family. Isaac did try a few jobs, once as a conductor on the Coney Island Railroad and briefly at a local bank. Mostly, he could be found on the top floor of the boardinghouse, reading.

My mother's mother, Rose, had a different story. She boldly left home to attend medical school in Lemberg (now Lviv, Ukraine), where she studied to become a midwife. I found it very romantic when she told me that her suitor and future husband Jacob was so distressed when he thought she had abandoned him that he climbed up on a chair with a rope in hand and threatened to hang himself. Of course, she returned, and they too made the journey to America. When she and Jacob moved into an apartment house in the Bronx, she continued to deliver babies until my grandfather earned enough money to support them and put a stop to her working life. She never told me if she had minded, but it was very important to Rose that her own daughter, Tillie, have a reliable profession of her own.

My mother, a sweet-faced, blue-eyed and talented pianist had hoped for a musical career, but she gave that up when she married her Abe and became a schoolteacher. It wasn't possible to resist the handsome young lawyer who travelled up to the Bronx each weekend to woo her, wearing spats that he borrowed from a friend, whose family owned a more prosperous bathhouse in Coney. Tillie's older brother, Dave, was also musical, a violin prodigy who never quite made it to the concert stage, but he did get to work as concertmaster at the fabled Roxy Theater in Manhattan for many years, and for a kid like me, walking into that movie palace was heaven brought down to Seventh Avenue and 50th Street.

I'm not technically a Coney Island baby since my first years were spent in a comfortable house with a Spanish tile roof and a flower garden in Sea Gate, the gated community at the tip of Coney Island.

Its development dates back to the 1890s, when Norton's Point Land Company bought all of the land and sold property to several wealthy Manhattan families, including the Vanderbilts and Morgans. In my father's telling, it was a not-so-well-kept secret that the rich men installed their mistresses by the ocean and that the security guards at the gates were there solely to call ahead to warn the men that their wives were minutes away. His authority on this bit of history rests on the fact that Kalina's Baths was just a few blocks away, and a curious boy could see this unfolding with his own eyes, along with the posted sign, "No dogs or Jews allowed."

But that exclusion was gone by the late 1930s when my parents pooled what little cash they had with Rose and Jacob and set out to build a life together. It all came crashing down when, a few years later, my father was diagnosed with scleroderma and advised by a doctor to lie in the sun. So he packed up a small bag and took a train to Florida, leaving my mother, who was pregnant with their third child, to cope. He sent letters home with the little money he was able to earn as a luggage salesman and complained about having to eat Spam, which horrified my kosher grandparents.

My mother, left on her own and in a panic about money, made the decision to sell the house and rent a tenement flat above a butcher's shop on Mermaid Avenue so the family could survive on her meager substitute teacher's income. I hated that cockroach-infested apartment the second we walked through the door and, being a child, couldn't really understand what was going on. We were only ten blocks away from my beloved house and garden in Sea Gate, but the chain-link fence and its gate manned by security guards contrived to make me believe that we had been banned for some hidden crime. To make matters worse, a Rabbi Galinsky and his sons lived one floor above us and were continuously fighting. The sounds of their raised voices came down through an opening in the ceiling right below their toilet, so we had the added embarrassment of hearing noises that should have remained strictly private.

But my dear mother never complained. She just pushed on, getting up at 6AM to fill our brown paper lunch bags with sandwiches and apples, take a bus to Stillwell Avenue, then a train to Public School 253 in Brighton Beach, teach her third graders reading, writing and arithmetic until 3PM, return to Mermaid Avenue and stop at the grocer, butcher and baker, cook our dinner, clean up and, if she could stay awake, work on her lesson plan. I can still hear her sigh of relief when she took off her girdle the second she was home. My father, who had returned after many months with his health restored, had quite the opposite routine: he came home from work, had his shot of Seagram's V.O., stretched out on the couch for a nap, had dinner with the family and kept Tillie company, drying the dishes as she scrubbed away. I doubt he ever cooked a meal on his own. It certainly never seemed to occur to either of them that there was something not quite fair with the arrangement.

In spite of their very different temperaments — my mother self-contained and private, my father quick to get angry — they were in love. I took after my father, and we were the ones who got into heated arguments ending with his calling me "a lousy rotten kid" and my demanding of my mother that she leave *him* at once. With a sigh, she would remind me that he had never been shown any affection as a child and that I might try to be a little more understanding about why he was never physically affectionate with me. But, alas, I didn't know how. It always caused me pangs of jealousy to watch a friend's father give her a hug. Those rare times when his love for me would shine through were at older cousins' weddings when, quite tipsy and with a shy smile on his face, he would ask me to dance and tell me what a beautiful girl I was.

David, my older brother, never even tried to hide his dim view of me. I was that pesky kid sister he had been ordered to take care of after school and most of Saturday. That was the day my mother cleaned house, and she wanted us all out of her way, including my father, who spent the day hanging out at the local Democratic Club, while David took me off to a movie theater to see our hero, Smilin' Jack, outwit his enemies before the double bill began. *Frankenstein* so terrified me that I went to hide in the ladies' room, checking every stall to make sure Frankenstein's monster wasn't waiting for me there. For months afterwards, when I went to bed in the room I shared with my baby brother Robert, I cowered under my blanket, sure that I heard the monster on the fire escape outside our window coming to snatch me away just as he had snatched and killed the little girl in the movie.

On summer Saturdays, when it was too beautiful to sit inside the dark theater, David meted out his babysitting punishment by ordering me into the front seat of the infamous Cyclone roller coaster to delight at my misery as we dropped straight down, with my stomach in free fall. I had to swear never to tell, or he'd make me go up again or play Bloody Knucks, a card game in which the loser gets his (inevitably her) knuckles raked hard with the deck. I never told my parents, and so David remained prized by them as my protector. They would have been traumatized if I told them he had me lie down on their bed when they were out one evening and climbed on top of me. I thought it was a game until he hoisted my skirt and tried to penetrate me. I pushed him away and ran off, confused, not really understanding what had just happened or almost happened. I had mumbled something like "It tickles, stop." It's small wonder that shortly after the incident, I developed a new terror after seeing the movie *Bewitched*. The young heroine had an evil self that lived inside her, commanding her to kill people with a knife. For weeks after, sitting at the dinner table was a torment; I was convinced that an evil twin was alive inside me and might force my hand to pick up the table knife and strike out. If only I had dared tell someone about David's abusive behavior, it might have saved me from therapy years later, but he was counting on my habit of keeping his secrets, making them my secrets too.

Far safer was going to my grandparents' apartment around the corner. I can easily remember every detail of the place, from the worn-down steps leading up to the third floor and the *mezuzah* on the doorframe to the blue satin sofa where Grandpa Jake often sat watching grainy wrestling matches on TV and excitedly calling out his encouragement or scorn in Yiddish much as Grandma Rose loudly cursed the villains in Westerns (her favorites) at our local movie theater. Sitting beside her, I was so mortified, I always slid down low in my seat, sure that my classmates were in the rows behind and laughing at us.

In the early 1940s, Coney was an all-white neighborhood evenly divided between Italians and Jews whose children mingled at grammar school, one of those factory-looking brick buildings, just a few blocks west of Nathan's Famous Hot Dogs. Our teachers were all female and Irish, very strict but not unkind, and did their best to educate us in the Palmer method of penmanship, the multiplication tables and the three branches of government. When America entered the war after the bombing of Pearl Harbor, we dutifully filed into the dingy yellow hallways once a week and seated ourselves against the wall for air-raid drills, a serious business heightened by the constant rumors of German submarines sighted along our Coney Island shore.

I became best friends with shy Phyllis Lieberman who lived just a block away, but my mother was uneasy about it. Her father was a reputed gangster who was never home, and her mother kept a Doberman Pinscher chained to a tall metal radiator whenever she left us alone in the apartment. The whole place had an air of sin and mystery, especially after we opened a drawer next to her parents' bed and found a deck of pornographic playing cards made extra dirty for me because the naked men still wore their black socks and shoes as they straddled the women. Phyllis and I pronounced them "icky," but we couldn't stop ourselves from looking. One afternoon, the Doberman must have sensed something amiss. He yanked himself free of his radiator chain and came after us, barking ferociously. Petrified, we jumped onto her parents' bed and screamed our heads off. Luckily, the dog didn't follow. When Mrs. Lieberman came home, she took one look at the exposed cards, calmly put them away and told me to leave. Phyllis never told me what happened afterwards.

When the Allied forces at last defeated Hitler's army in Europe, Coney Island exploded in joy. My mother tied up my braids with colored ribbons and decorated baby brother Robert's stroller with red, white and blue streamers and let me push him through the crowds as fireworks lit up the sky. Up and down the Island, every street had its own spontaneous block party, the grownups drunk on alcohol and victory, the kids chasing each other around until they fell asleep, exhausted, on the stoops.

The war had lasted for half of my young life, and now that we were safe from the threat of German U-boats, my parents allowed me to go down to the Bowery rides with just my girlfriends. We spent whole days at George C. Tilyou's Steeplechase, The Funny Place, a giant enclosed park right off the Boardwalk. My favorite was the Horse Race, a thrilling ride on rails round the perimeter of the park on wooden horses. Upon dismounting, we had to travel through a dimly lit tunnel that abruptly dropped us onto the Blowhole Theater stage where blasts of air shot up through vents for the sole purpose of blowing up girls' skirts so the audience, seated above, could roar with laughter. I'll never forget being shocked in the rear with a cattle prod by a scary clown as I tried to escape across the Battleship Roll, an undulating section of the floor, only to be caught by a second clown wielding a slapstick that left me humiliated. But once I scrambled off the stage, I not only joined the crowd to laugh at the next batch of victims but also rode the horses over and over, in spite of, or mostly because of, the terrifying ending.

And always there was the ever-looming presence of the Kalinas, my father and his brothers and sisters, all eight of them, who met most Saturday nights to play gin rummy and quarrel as though they were still children, while my many cousins and I stayed out of their way by jumping up on beds to play King of the Hill. Uncle Victor, a shoe manufacturer with a perennial cigar hanging from his lower lip, would bet my little brother a quarter that he couldn't be quiet for more than five minutes and always won. The four sisters were uniformly homely, their daughters beautiful. The sweetest among them, Aunt Minnie, had the good fortune to marry a banker. Like my father, she drank too much at weddings, would wax sentimental with her nieces and make gifts of the expensive jewelry she was wearing until, at the close of the evening, her husband would go around our kids' table politely asking us to surrender the stash. Then there was Aunt Bella of the jowls, dubbed "Bella the Boss" by my brother David, although the real boss in the family was my Uncle Emil, the cardiologist. Just a few inches over five feet, he exerted so much authority among his siblings that when my father suffered what would be his last and fatal heart attack in his late sixties, my mother unthinkingly drove him straight to Emil's hospital in Queens. That forty-five minute trip cost my father his life. My mother never forgave herself.

As was expected of me, I was a good girl at school, getting all A's and a check mark next to "works and plays well with others" on my report cards, graduating from sixth grade with a civics award for writing an essay about racial integration. I was so shocked when my name was called that I tripped going up to the stage to receive my prize, a slim red book, *Call Me Charley,* about a Black newspaper boy encountering prejudice in an all-white neighborhood. In the flyleaf was an inscription: "To Joyce, with gratitude for your understanding of our country and its people. A. Loretta Callahan, Principal of P.S. 80, Congratulations!" Unearned praise for an eleven-year-old who had rarely seen a Black person and whose insular world was rife with prejudice.

After my father began to bring in more income from his law practice, my parents moved us out of the tenement flat on Mermaid Avenue to a quieter side street, renting the top floor of a two-story building with a small garden that was tended to by our Italian landlords who lived below and ran a small deli on the corner. It was a step up, no roaches, my own bedroom, but it seemed the mice had felt free to tag along, and I would instantly run from the room at the sight of one scurrying across the linoleum.

When it was time to enroll in a large junior high, I found myself in a class with the girls who had been my neighbors in Sea Gate, still living in the same big houses with fathers who had made a killing in the black market during the war. The girls never asked about where I lived, and if I wanted to be friends with them I had to bicycle through the Gate on my old rusty Schwinn. The leaders of the clique, Toby and Judy, seemed so sure of themselves I always felt somehow inferior around them. I would be in an agony of suspense on Thursdays, never knowing if I would be invited to join them for some weekend activity as subversive as eating BLT sandwiches (non-kosher and forbidden) at the Sea Gate Sweetshop or to a sleepover which made me aware of the abundance in their homes. My mouth watered at the sight of their bedroom drawers filled with cashmere sweaters of every shade.

It seems like sex was always on our minds. The childish games we played — Spin-the-Bottle and Post Office — aroused our curiosity, as did the used condoms that littered the school's empty sports stands. I got my first look at a real penis while walking home alone after class one afternoon when a car pulled over to the curb and a man leaned out asking for directions, his trousers unzipped and jerking off. Petrified, I ran all the way home, afraid he would reach out and pull me into his car. That wasn't the last time I saw the sleazy side of sexual arousal, the subway being a favorite spot for men to expose themselves to young girls. I finally had my first real kiss one warm summer night on the beach from a boy named Harvey. When I pulled away to complain of something pressing against my stomach, he apologized (it was too dark to see his probably red face) and told me it was his belt buckle, and I believed him. All was revealed when my best friend Deena and I surreptitiously read the banned *The Amboy Dukes* when her parents were away and got so excited reading about how "it" was done that we lay down on their big bed and fondled each other's small breasts while kissing passionately.

When we tired of watching the boys play softball in the park, we spent our summer days swimming, the only sport considered appropriate for girls our age, and retreated into books that took me adventuring to far-off places. I longed to explore the magical forest depicted in *Green Mansions,* a novel inhabited by Rima, a girl who could talk with birds or set sail for the China conjured in Pearl Buck's *The Good Earth*. Those novels set me to thinking about becoming an archeologist or an anthropologist, though I wasn't yet sure of the difference between the two.

two

I WAS ABOUT TO graduate from Lincoln High School (or "Stinkin' Linkin'" as we fondly called it) in the Class of '53, and I was smitten with theater, having just landed the ingénue part of the aspiring ballerina Essie in George S. Kaufman's comedy, *You Can't Take It with You*. Fortunately for me, Essie was talentless, and so, with just a few ballet classes to learn first and second position, I was able to carry it off. It was so thrilling to be part of a theater group that I was more than eager to repeat the experience. My parents greatly enjoyed the show and assumed that I would move on to perform while studying at Brooklyn College, my dad's alma mater, but I waged an all-out war against it.

To my dismay, the only other school not in commuting distance they would even consider for me was Brandeis University. A Jewish world was the last place on earth I wanted to be. My negative feelings about religion hadn't changed since I was five years old, sitting with my Grandma Rose up in the balcony reserved for women in the Sea Gate synagogue. It was Rosh Hashanah, the air hot with a mix of perfume and perspiration, and I felt I might suffocate under the piles of shawls and fur jackets strewn about. Even worse, I was trapped behind the curtain that closed off any view of the rabbi and davening men below. I became so outraged that a girl couldn't be where the action was that I rushed out into the fresh air and down the fire escape stairs. I think it was in that moment that I vowed never to set foot in a house of worship again.

Predictably, when the time came for me to choose a college, it meant very little to my self-involved self that when Brandeis had opened its doors barely five years earlier, it offered opportunities

11

to students and professors who had been turned away by most colleges and universities due to anti-Semitic quotas, which had begun in the early 1920s when schools like Harvard and Yale saw a steady increase in the number of Jewish students qualifying for admittance and were afraid it would "drive the gentiles away."

I don't know who was more ill at ease, my parents or me that fall day, when they left me in that girls-only dorm in Massachusetts, a Normandy-style castle that the Brandeis founders inherited when they purchased property just outside Boston. Except for the time my father spent in Florida when he was sick, neither of them had travelled outside of New York. I lucked out in my assigned roommate, Nita, but, to my disappointment, she would be sporting a large pear-shaped diamond ring within months and leave college by the end of our freshman year to get married, as would Deena, my best friend from Sea Gate. I would miss them both terribly.

I had excelled in biology and was fully expecting to major in that field, thinking it good grounding for a future archeologist and, if not for the condescension of a chemistry teacher, I might have spent my life hunting fossils in Tanzania, like my heroine, Meave Leakey. To my dismay, I received a D on my first organic chemistry exam, made far worse when the professor handed back our tests and asked me to wait until the other students had left. Barely hiding his disdain, he informed me that I clearly wasn't cut out to be a scientist and "might consider" withdrawing from his class. I was the only girl in that class, and with no adviser to warn me that most students struggle with the subject in their freshman year, I left his classroom in shock, with plans for my future in tatters. My French professor was so very charismatic that without giving it much thought, I switched majors and landed in the Comparative Literature Department. The course work was far easier and gave me time to start acting in one play after another, intensifying what had been just a fancy in high school, especially after I landed the female lead in the annual musical comedy, twin princesses, one wicked with flaming red hair (I kept her curly wig in my pocket), the other a goody-goody and not nearly as much fun to play. When

I look at the press photos in an album my mother kept, I can't believe it's me, arms spread wide, blithely singing away.

By the middle of that first winter at Brandeis, Deena proudly told me that she was no longer a virgin. Not satisfied with being left behind, I felt I had to follow suit and promptly began my first love affair with an older student who was Irish and had a motorcycle. Bob's parents owned a lake cottage nearby where we able to sneak away in the early evenings before I had to sign back in to my dorm before curfew. I can still smell the soft air on my face as we sped through the night with my arms cinched tight around him. We even managed to get summer jobs at the same inn on Cape Cod — he as a bartender and I as a waitress — with my mother and father believing I was working there with a friend. I wasn't in the habit of lying to them, but I knew how dismayed they would be, particularly my mother, if she even suspected that her good girl was having sex before marriage, especially with a non-Jew. It was easier to just cover it up.

Perhaps she helped by being so very private about her own body — I never once saw my mother naked — and she rarely ever talked about sex. I certainly never told her, or anyone else until years later, that when I broke off with Bob the following year and began seeing someone else, he burst into my off-campus bedroom in the middle of the night in a jealous rage, reeking of alcohol, and raped me. The poor fellow I was with ran off in a panic the second Bob broke down the door, and I couldn't blame him; he and his family had escaped Nazi storm troopers just ten years before. I do remember lying there with Bob on top of me afterwards, sobbing his apologies as I gazed at the dawn light coming through the thin bedroom shade, feeling separated from my own body, not able to speak. I had been transported into a parallel universe of violence. Hearing the street outside come to life — a dog barking, a car engine starting up — I knew that the inhabitants of that everyday universe weren't remotely aware of what was taking place barely a hundred feet away.

As I try to recall how I felt in the hours and days that followed, my memory plays tricks with me. My first impulse is to say that

I felt overwhelmed with shame. But it's entirely possible that I'm projecting backwards feelings that I now think I was supposed to have. Knowing how I respond to being hurt, I think it more likely that my overriding feeling was anger. It certainly never occurred to me to report Bob to the police, and, even if I had, they would have done nothing other than insinuate that, by being promiscuous, I had brought this upon myself. I do know that I sought refuge in burying myself in French novels, particularly loving Colette, and, much like the music hall heroine of her tale *La Vagabonde*, I longed to live my life travelling with a theater troupe far, far away. It was the first flickering of a desire to make acting my career.

When my parents gave their blessing to my idea of studying in Paris the following year, I was amazed and completely overwhelmed with gratitude, knowing how uneasy they were already about my wandering beyond their little corner of Brooklyn. Dressed in their Sunday best, my family waved good-bye to me from Manhattan's Pier 92 as I, and a contingent of Sweetbriar College young ladies in white gloves, excitedly set sail on a crisp fall afternoon aboard the SS *Mauretania* for France. Fortunately, there were male students from Yale in the program as well, and those five days of flirting, lounging on deck chairs under soft blankets and gazing at the white-capped waves while listening for the jingly tune of the steward's bell fore-telling his arrival with a tray of hot bouillon mugs cast an enchant-ment over me that air travel will never replicate. The day we were to reach land, I scrambled out of bed at dawn so I could watch the boat slowly dock at *Le Havre, an*d, as if cued by a film director, a man riding his bike, a fresh baguette under his arm, suddenly appeared on the pier below and waved his beret in welcome.

Once settled in Paris, I was assigned housing with two other girls in the apartment of a formidable Frenchwoman who unnerved us, the architectural historian Simone Gille-Delafon, who had an émigré Russian male servant always scurrying down the corridors to do her bidding. I can still hear her screaming, "Basil, Basil!" in her shrill voice that woke me on many a morning. Madame's husband had been an officer in Petain's Vichy government, something she never talked about, nor did she show much concern about our comings and goings.

On our first night, my roommate Janet and I set out to explore as many streets in the Latin Quarter as we could under the spell of *la vie bohème*, wandering for hours amidst all its beauty, finally stopping at a small corner cafe on the *Boul' Mich'* and, with the kind of style we had seen in gangster movies, swaggered up to the counter and ordered *deux cognacs*, ready to slap our few francs down. Standing next to us were a group of Swedes in their twenties who were highly amused. I remember every one of them to this day — Stig, Jan and the beautiful Brigitta, a Garbo lookalike — because I became their little American mascot, their *Kalinka* (little red berry in Russian), following them from café to café for months. Not only drunk in love with all of them but also drunk on the Calvados we consumed most nights, sobering up at *Les Halles* near dawn with bowls of steaming hot onion soup bubbling with cheese. I was entranced with their larger than life emotional turmoil, their tales of past loves and near-suicides most often expressed in gory detail. Jan even rolled up his sweater to show me his wrist scars to prove they were true.

All three were painters, the first artists I had ever known, and lovers of the movies, taking me to the Cinémathèque Française where Henri Langlois devoted whole months to individual directors or countries. There for the first time I heard the word "film" used instead of "movie" in conversation and discovered that the varied styles of directing we viewed were exciting to dissect. In fact, it had never even occurred to me that each movie did have a different style. Most intriguing was a new film magazine, *Cahiers du Cinema*, and I was surprised to see that a young reviewer I had never heard of, Francois Truffaut, was treating Hitchcock's *Rear Window* and *Spellbound*, which I had thought of as merely Saturday night entertainment, with the seriousness of a postgraduate student analyzing a Shakespeare sonnet. Here was Truffaut making the startling argument that a director with a distinctive style should be held in the same high regard as first-rate authors, or *auteurs*, an appellation he would later claim for himself with his memorable *Jules and Jim*.

My being there to study French literature was a ruse; I just wanted to soak up everything Parisian and be as much like its inhabitants as possible. To my adolescent eyes, its citizens were all heroic survivors of World War II. It was only later, after seeing Marcel Ophuls's searing 1968 documentary, *The Sorrow and the Pity*, that I would learn that many of them were willfully forgetting that they had stood silently by just ten years earlier as their Jewish neighbors were being carted away by the Nazis. But that knowledge was in the future. It didn't take more than a few days for Janet and me to decide that we had to take at least one course for credit at the Sorbonne, the seat of ancient learning, so we signed up for a course on Aristotle's *Metaphysics*, which was a disaster. The course would have been difficult enough in English, but in French it was hopeless to truly understand *la Science de l'être en tant qu'être* so we started skipping classes. When exam time came, the professor took pity on us and told us, in advance, he would query us on book *Lambda* and offered private exams in his office to spare us embarrassment. I volunteered to double-check the English translation of the word lambda so we could be sure we were cramming the correct section.

After a few days of hard studying and little sleep, we knew the chapter by heart in both languages and set out feeling secure enough to believe we would do well. After a half-hour wait in one of the Sorbonne's dark hallways, the professor opened his door and motioned for Janet to go in first. She was out in less than a minute. As she flew past, I could hear her muttering in a not-too-muted voice, "You shmuck, we read the wrong book!" My stomach dropped as the professor smiled at me with a cat smile and motioned that it was my turn. But fortune smiled on me. The questions all related to Aristotle's theories of the planets, which I had studied in a freshman science course and remembered enough to earn an undeserved A.

To celebrate, I went along with my Swedish pals to a party hosted by the Swedish ambassador's son at the embassy while his mother was away. At midnight, each glass was filled to the brim with aquavit, every glass was raised in a toast, then wanting to be like the Swedes, I sang out *Skol* and drank it in one swallow. Within minutes,

I and all the other guests had passed out cold. When I awoke some hours later, the ambassador's son was unbuttoning my blouse. He was so terribly woozy I easily pushed him off and tiptoed around the beautiful young people fast asleep on the floor as if they were in a fairytale. Somehow I got back to my apartment, head still spinning, flopped onto my bed and fell into a drunk's sleep.

When I woke up with a brain-shattering headache, I resolved to reform my ways. I gave up my nightly round of the bars, which freed me to spend more nights at the Cinémathèque with a new friend, Ada, a young Israeli *sabra* who, like the prickly pear the Hebrew word derives from to denote Jews born in Israel, was tough on the outside but as sweet as could be inside. On trips to museums, Ada taught me how to look at paintings in a new way, urging me to be more aware of how the best painters selected the light's direction and intensity to enhance their work. It led me to pay attention ever after to how directors employed it in so many of the films I most admired, especially the black-and-white movies of the 1940s such as *Double Indemnity* and *The Maltese Falcon*, where low-key lighting created shadows and gave the viewer a sense that danger lurked just around the corner.

I also became fascinated with the mime Jean-Louis Barrault, the star of Marcel Carne's *Les Enfants du Paradis*. Wanting to learn more about how he moved with such fluid motion, I discovered that his teacher, Étienne Decroux, lived in Paris and was allowing newcomers to join his class for a small weekly fee. Dressed in loose white pants and a sleeveless white T-shirt, *le maitre* played the role of the imperious taskmaster to perfection, overseeing our feeble attempts to control each part of our body separately, one joint at a time, the key to a mime's movement. By the time June came, I had barely made any progress and wrote my parents that I absolutely had to remain in Paris if I had any hope of becoming a mime. With her usual wry humor, my mother replied that, with regrets, the family couldn't continue to support me in my chosen career but wished me the best.

I was on board the SS *Ryndam* sailing home to New York within a week, a very unhappy young woman. My parents walked right past me on the Hoboken dock. I had gained so much weight on Basil's cooking and drinking with my Swedes that they didn't recognize me, a young snob who now disdained everything American, having bought into the cliché that by comparison to France, the epitome of culture and style, mid-1950s America was a cultural wasteland. One look at the endless fins of a new Chevrolet was enough to convince me.

I continued my love affair with all things French when I returned to Brandeis in the fall and saw lots of foreign films at the Brattle Theater in Cambridge, renting a room in a nearby boardinghouse and commuting to classes by train. My father had high hopes of my following in his footsteps into law school, especially after an aptitude test showed my abilities lay there. He even held out a promise that he could get me a job as a Brooklyn assistant D.A. It all sounded glamorous, with shades of my heroine, Nancy Drew, girl detective, thrown in. He was disappointed when I said that a law career didn't much appeal to me, especially after David had turned him down and was now a Julliard student. He wasn't overly happy when I admitted that I was now determined to become a professional actress and see where it would take me.

The last person on my mind was Bob, and I was surprised when he showed up one evening on my doorstep. Flustered, I invited him into my room where he wasted little time in telling me that he was still in love with me and leaning down, kissed me. Whether it was just lust after a year of chastity or plain stupidity on my part, I was having sex with him within minutes, the old deep attraction still there. As soon as it was over, I was so troubled by what I had just done I could barely wait for him to leave. The next day, I sent Bob a note telling him I had made a terrible mistake, that I could never be with him again. "Please forgive me." It was the last time I ever saw him. A month later, with my period overdue, I went into a panic; a test confirmed that I was pregnant. Worse, there was no one I dared make my confidant to ease my terror. Certainly not Bob, who was Catholic and might want to marry me and have the child, and least of all my mother. I foolishly continued to assume that she needed protection from the idea of me having sex and would be horrified that her daughter was even contemplating an abortion. It was not only illegal, my head was also filled with terrifying stories of women who had bled to death at the hands of back alley quacks using filthy knitting needles to terminate their pregnancies. Even if I dared have one, I had absolutely no idea about where I might obtain one, let alone pay for it.

Desperation drove me. I didn't want to be a mother before I had a chance to have a life of my own. I can't remember how, but I finally got the name of a Manhattan doctor who agreed to perform the abortion for $300, a princely sum that I had to borrow from Toby, my Sea Gate friend, who kindly asked no questions. Christmas vacation was fast approaching, which gave me an excuse to be home and close to the city. All I recall is that it was a Saturday, that I was alone and petrified as I climbed a darkened staircase somewhere on the East Side to reach the doctor's office, that a kindly nurse was present, that the doctor was eager for me to leave as soon as he had done his job of scraping the lining of my uterus, that I was woozy but not bleeding excessively. Only when the deed was done did I allow myself to admit that I had been insane to trust my body to a complete stranger.

On the subway ride home, I felt so hot all over my body that it was a relief to press my face against the cool glass and stare into the dark black tunnel, praying for the lights in the train to dim to darkness as well and hide me from my own reflection, so distressed by what I had just done. When I finally arrived home, my parents were concerned that I seemed unusually pale and sent me off to bed, my loving mother visiting occasionally to stroke my head. They fell for my story that I had been at the Metropolitan Museum with visiting college friends and had overdone showing them around, which only served to increase my misery. I was now their full-blown deceitful daughter. When I woke up the next morning, to my immense relief, I was completely pain-free and relieved to have escaped unharmed, ready to move on with my life and knowing how fortunate I was to have friends with money who could help me.

Back on campus, an envelope containing my fall semester grades was waiting in my mailbox. They were so terrible that I was shocked into action and settled into the routine of studying, trying my best to resist the temptation of the darkened movie theaters. June came and, with it, Brandeis's sixth graduation ceremony held in the university's new outdoor amphitheater. Though my parents were excited to see me receive my diploma, these two children of immigrants gazed down in awe to the stage below as Harry Truman and Aaron Copeland, in ceremonial robes, were awarded Honorary Degrees. But it was Eleanor Roosevelt who truly made them feel in the presence of greatness when she rose to speak. With a lingering glow, we all headed back to New York City.

I had been accepted as a full-time student at the Neighborhood Playhouse in Manhattan, the best acting school in the country, headed by Sandford Meisner, with Martha Graham to teach us movement. Her whacks to my stomach when I failed to hold it in tightly were considered a privilege. Sandy did his best to teach us his now legendary method of "living truthfully under imaginary circumstances" by staying in the moment and responding to what you got from an acting partner instead of predetermining an end result for the scene. His only troubling and somewhat sadistic rule was forbidding students to smoke in his class even as he blithely chain-smoked away. As a pack-a-day Camel smoker, I found it a mild torture to enter his classroom.

But I had more serious difficulties. I couldn't afford to live in Manhattan and had to move home to live with my parents, which wasn't easy after four years of living on my own. The subway ride was close to an hour, not including the inexplicable delays that caused the trains to stop in between stations with no way to know if we would be stuck there for one minute or forever. What started as irritation turned into full-blown anxiety attacks, although I didn't know to call them that. It was a feeling of desperation, a need to flee so extreme I wanted to die.

The fear of "it" happening again began to control my life. My stomach was so upset that I dreaded going to the bathroom at the

Playhouse when other girls were in there, deeply ashamed of their hearing my explosions. I finally avoided the subway and rode to town with my father, squeezed in the car's back seat between two and sometimes three of his colleagues. With too few paying clients, he had closed his solo law practice to clerk for a State Supreme Court judge near the Brooklyn Bridge. Those trips proved worse than the subway since we were usually stuck in traffic jams and I couldn't tell my emotionally distant father what I was going through. One snowy day in late winter, unable to cope any longer, I gave up and told Mr. Meisner that I needed a break, mumbling some reason I can't remember, and he assured me that I could return whenever I wanted to. I fled back to Cambridge, leaving my worried parents behind. The anxiety attacks disappeared as soon as I boarded the Amtrak train for Boston. I was back in control.

three

THERE WEREN'T MANY jobs available for a young woman of twenty-one with a degree in comparative literature, and I didn't want to learn dictation and become a secretary. Actually, I was afraid that, if I did learn, I would irrevocably land on the slippery slope to nowhere. I found a job at a nearby French restaurant where I worked most nights, hoisting heavy metal trays, but I was at a total loss about what to do with my life. I had been so certain that I wanted to be an actress that I now felt like a failure before I had even begun. The only consolation lay in finally being free to read my way through the great Russian novels — the gloomy Dostoevsky was my favorite — without having to write a paper. One day, I ran into a classmate, Paula Kelley, a blonde with a flair for drama, whom I had barely known at Brandeis. She was also unhappy with the job she had found and we fantasized about starting a business of our own. The romance of Paris hadn't worn off, and I suggested we open a continental-style café with wooden racks of foreign-language newspapers and an array of drinks, from Italian espresso to Turkish coffee. Paula had saved a thousand dollars and, once again, my cash-strapped but devoted parents came through, agreeing to send me the same amount, this time as a loan.

We immediately began scouting empty stores in Cambridge, finding nothing suitable, until we read that Fournier's Used Furniture Emporium was going out of business. It was located on Mt. Auburn Street, about five blocks from Harvard Square, which, in 1958, was a seedy low-rent district. We rushed over and peered through the gigantic plate glass windows. It was perfect. Mr. Cahaly, the owner of the neighboring deli, informed us that the landlord was a Miss

Bertha Cohen whose office was in a grand apartment building she owned along the Charles River near the Harvard boathouse. In fact, Miss Bertha Cohen owned a great deal of property throughout the Boston area. I was later to learn from her obit in the *Harvard Crimson* that Bertha had come to this country as a young Polish immigrant with little money and began work as a milliner in the old Chandler Company department store in Boston. Living frugally, she saved enough money from her weekly salary to launch a real estate business that left her, as her many sneering foes used to say, "that Yid who practically owns Harvard Square."

Guided only by a small sign with the word "Office" and a gilt hand pointing the direction, the kind you'd buy at a hardware store for a dime, Paula and I stumbled our way through a dimly lit basement hallway. If you've read Dickens, you will have a good sense of what we found. In a cramped office, seated at an ancient roll-top desk covered with dozens of uncashed checks, sat the elderly Mrs. Cahill, Bertha's secretary. Bertha must have heard our voices, and she came out of an even smaller office to inquire, shabbily dressed, belying her reputed wealth. She might have been forty or ninety. When we stated our business, she refused to talk further with us, saying that she never rented her commercial properties to twenty-one-year-olds. But our enterprising spirits must have touched her because she finally relented and signed a lease, though not before exhorting us young ladies to follow her example by saving our pennies. As if to illustrate her point, Bertha proudly opened a closet filled with shards of broken glass she had collected from her various properties under repair. We were speechless. After that, I took to delivering our monthly rent checks in person on the chance she would be in, so I could hear a few more of her rambling stories, and one afternoon she surprised me by inviting me up to her apartment for tea. She had a matter she wanted to discuss with me in private.

The place was pure Victorian, every inch of space crammed with porcelain lamps, painted vases and china figurines of lads and lasses in pale pastels. She served us in bone china cups and asked if I would consider working for her. I was speechless . . . and touched . . .

and tempted, picturing myself as a real estate mogul with thousand-dollar bills strewn around my feet. I felt a strange kinship with her, so it was with real regret that I thanked my landlady as warmly as I could and never visited with her again. When the Boston papers announced that she had died without a will, leaving an estate valued at twenty million dollars that distant relatives were squabbling over, I felt sad for her strange and lonely life. But that was hardly on my mind the afternoon Paula and I left that basement office, ready to tackle the universe.

With the energy of youth, we set out to put up three plywood walls to enclose a kitchen, repair the cracks in the ceiling, install light fixtures and fix the basement toilet, all with the helpful advice of an amused staff at our local hardware store. Painting every surface was the easy part. By talking endless numbers of people into giving us credit we secured four hot plates (since we had no stove), secondhand tables and chairs, cups and saucers, serving trays and teaspoons. I even got to make use of my dressmaking skills that all junior high girls had to learn in Home Economics, sewing drapes for the large plate glass windows on the same small Singer sewing machine I still had with me. Taken all in all, the work was a great boost to our delusional belief that we could do anything we set our minds to, that is anything except coming up with a name for our café, and finally we settled on the address, 47 Mt. Auburn Street, barely in time to get our first menu printed. A week before we were set to open, a senior at Harvard dropped in and asked if we would like to have music at the grand event. Steve Kuhn was already an accomplished jazz pianist around Boston so we happily accepted.

I almost didn't make it to the opening. It started with my waking up with terrible stomach pains. I assumed they were menstrual cramps, the fierce kind that disabled me every month, but, as the day wore on, they became so unbearable I just wanted to die. I was alone, without a telephone or fan (the outside temperature 95 degrees) in a third-floor bedroom I was renting in a private house. Paula saved my life. Worried that I hadn't shown up for a meeting, she climbed up to my room and found me burning up with fever. All I wanted my friend to do was get a gun and shoot me, but she insisted on half-carrying me to her car and driving to her family's physician nearby. The quick-witted Dr. O'Brien took one look at me and said that my appendix had probably burst, that I would need to have my stomach pumped out ASAP or I would see my wish to die come true. The last thing I remember hearing before surgery was the word "peritonitis," followed by a blissful release from pain as a nurse injected me with sodium pentothal as an aide rushed my gurney down a corridor to the operating room.

I woke to the sound of a voice saying, "If you move, I'll smack you." A fierce-looking nurse was standing over me, attaching a drip line into my arm, my anxious parents hovering behind her. When Dr. O'Brian strode in, he insisted that I get out of bed so we could "take a little stroll in the park." Abe and Tillie were aghast as he waltzed me down the hallway, both of us delighting in their shocked expressions as he told stories about his time as an army surgeon and noted that his soldiers were healing faster if they were on their feet within hours of major surgery. He proved right, and I was released in just a few days with a not very pretty, long vertical scar on my belly and his instructions, "*Don't* take it too easy, Kiddo."

Happily, our café was packed from day one — customers loved the music and tolerated our coffee. Paula and I were flying high. Young female entrepreneurs were such a rarity that, in addition to local articles about us and the café, one even appeared in the national fashion magazine *Mademoiselle*, which I mailed to my mother, happy that she would proudly add it to her scrapbook. It didn't take long to realize that we better keep the jazz going, and somehow Steve managed to complete his studies and play at the café until he graduated that spring. We forgot about being a pseudo-European style café and became a jazz destination. Although I had rarely listened to this music before, I was now becoming a true devotee. My parents drove up from New York to celebrate our success when a scene straight out of *Casablanca* erupted. Two Cambridge policemen came through the door, blew their whistles and announced, "This is a raid. The place is closed down." My fiery-tempered father started to protest. He was informed that his daughter was in violation of the city's blue laws enacted by the Puritan settlers and still in force, namely a prohibition against "live music with more than three stringed instruments while food was being served." They hit us with all sorts of violations. That we didn't have two toilets was one of them. Paula, the daughter of a local cop, was sure all they wanted was a bribe. She couldn't have been far from wrong since a nasty little lieutenant showed up not long after, put his foot up on a chair, and cited more violations. My favorite was that we were accused of running a call girl operation with Radcliffe "girls."

A novel solution presented itself within a month. With the help of a lawyer friend of Paula's, we filed and received approval for a nonprofit educational arts institution. Anyone who showed up at the door could put down one dollar and become a member of the renamed Club 47. Luckily, the Berklee School of Music was just across the river with a pool of talented musicians, and Alan Dawson, a superb drummer, and the equally talented Neves brothers took the stage. Our lively waitress, Helen Stephens, and her cousin Thelma once again moved to the jazz and waited on happy customers. After we locked up for the night, it didn't take long for Paula and me to settle into the routine of heading for our greasy spoon of choice, the Bickford in Harvard Square, or "the Bick" as it was affectionately known by hungry students and artists. We'd have our breakfast at midnight and then stroll back to the small apartment we shared close by. Once again, we hauled out our brushes and ladder to paint the walls and repair the broken ceiling fixtures. Those early days of running the club were days of deep satisfaction, of a kind I had never known before; the far-fetched dream of running our own business less than a year before had become a reality.

I took advantage of our new nonprofit status and started a Monday night film series with films rented from the Museum of Modern Art's collection. Although I had resumed taking acting classes in Boston, the idea of becoming a film director was beginning to take hold in my imagination, and I programmed the evenings much like those at the Cinémathèque in Paris, by country or by director, guided by the film history books I was beginning to devour. My favorite was *From Caligari to Hitler*, a study of German society during the pre-Nazi years that drew on such classics as *The Cabinet of Dr. Caligari* and *The Blue Angel* to examine the social and political reality of the time. I screened all of those films more than once so I could take notes on lighting and camera positions and was so Eurocentric that I never once considered renting anything made by an American. About a dozen people, mostly elderly and foreign, showed up to watch with me.

As I was putting away the projector and screen one Monday night, a most pleasant man introduced himself. His name was Peter Robinson, and he had come on behalf of a colleague, an MIT professor, who had a very talented daughter he wanted us to audition. As soon as he said, "folksinger," I hastily replied that we were a serious jazz club and had no interest in that sort of music. He gently persisted and asked if we would at least allow her to come the following Monday night when we were closed and audition for us. I reluctantly agreed. The next Monday night came and with it a teenage girl with long black hair framing her face and a guitar. She walked straight to our small stage, barefooted, and with no introductory patter began to sing. I almost fell off my chair hearing an uncannily beautiful voice fill the space.

It was Joan Baez, a freshman at Boston University. Paula and I just looked at each other and, in silent agreement, immediately offered the girl a spot on Wednesdays for ten dollars a night. The audience for her first performance consisted of her parents, her sister Mimi, her boyfriend, and a small group of friends, a total of eight patrons. Word spread quickly, and adoring, almost worshipful fans, crowded in, standing three-deep in the aisles. In no time, Club 47 became a mecca for the burgeoning folk music revival and, while remaining devoted jazz fans ourselves, we offered Joan the weekend nights, upping her fee to twenty-five dollars a night. Dozens of talented musicians had some of their earliest gigs there — Tom Rush, Jackie Washington, Judy Collins, Eric von Schmidt, the Charles River

Valley Boys, the list could fill the page. An unknown Bob Dylan also did a few sets.

I never got to know Joan personally during the time she performed at the Club. Even though I was only four years older, she made it clear from the beginning that Paula and I were Management and she was The Artist, and it hurt. We would just have to accept that she would be arrogant with us one minute and terrified the next, with stage fright so severe that while her enthralled audience waited for her to appear on stage, I would find her in the dark alley next to the club throwing up. It didn't help that her moody boyfriend, whom she was passionate about, was driving her crazy with jealousy.

As folk music took over more and more nights at Club 47, Paula and I continued to hang out late at night at George Wein's legendary jazz club, Storyville, on Tremont Street in Boston, where it wasn't unusual to thrill to Dave Brubeck or Stan Getz. Someone pointed out a pudgy man sitting alone at a table, surveying the scene. He was Albert Grossman, owner of the Chicago folk music club, Gate of Horn, and Odetta's manager. We went over, rather excited, and, introducing ourselves, told him about this amazing girl who was performing at our Cambridge club. He nodded, seemingly indifferent. But a few nights later, I noticed him sitting alone at the back of our club listening to Joan intently, no expression on his face. As was said of him later on when he was managing Bob Dylan and Peter, Paul & Mary, "He moved serenely and with deadly purpose like a barracuda circling shoals of fish." He left most ungraciously when Joan's set was over, without either a "hello" or a "thank you," and that was the last I saw of Mr. Grossman and the last I saw of Joan. A week later she was playing the Gate of Horn in Chicago, and she would soon make her first appearance at the Newport Folk Festival where she was invited, unannounced, to perform. It was pouring rain, but Paula and I barely noticed, we were so thrilled to be among the crowd that rose to their feet to wildly cheer the "barefoot Madonna."

One evening, I couldn't help but notice a handsome young man among the Club 47 crowd who was sitting alone and completely absorbed in the music. I was soon to learn his name, Amarjit Chopra, and hoped that he would return another night so that I could figure out a way to strike up a conversation. He did, and I took over serving him so that I could say a few words beyond, "Would you be needing anything else, sir?" As we began to talk, I was taken by what he told me about himself. Born and raised in northern India, he had recently graduated from MIT with a degree in engineering and intended to remain in the States and work for Transitron, one of the first high-tech companies on Boston's Route 128. I found him so appealing that we started seeing a lot of each other. If I found Amarjit appealing, I found the friends that he had made as an MIT undergrad equally so. All newly minted engineers, one was French, another Turkish, another Pakistani. My favorite was Mitko, a Bulgarian with a sense of whimsy not unlike his compatriot, Christo, who was beginning to create his astonishing land art installations and would later on show us models of them in his New York loft.

After two years of studying the films borrowed from the museum in New York, I was burning to find a way to become a film director myself, especially now that running the club was no longer engaging me with its routine work stocking the kitchen supplies, managing the small staff, filling endless orders for espresso and Turkish coffee, et cetera. I began to think about returning to France, as I still had such happy memories of living there. But it wasn't just happy memories that drew me. In the four years that had elapsed since I had studied there, the young *Cahiers du Cinema* critics had moved on to direct-ing their own films and were causing a stir worldwide, especially Jean-Luc Godard with his first feature, *Breathless*. The film would not open in the States until later in the year, but I had been reading about it, and I could have the chance to see it in the city where it had been made. So in spite of my growing attraction to Amarjit, I knew it was time to strike out on my own. I finally sold my share of the club to Paula for fifteen hundred dollars and, with the names of a few French film producers who had held out the likelihood of assistant jobs in my pocket, I bought a plane ticket to Paris.

I was filled with a sense of wonder and fear as the plane lifted off the runway at Idlewild Airport (renamed JFK after Kennedy's assassination) for what was one of the earliest commercial flights between New York and Paris that had tourist class seating and, on arrival, checked in to the dirt cheap hotel along the Left Bank where my friend Brigitta used to stay. I doubt I slept more than a few hours. I made my way to the first film studio on my list, full of high hopes. The producer was most welcoming for about five minutes and then proceeded to grab my ass. The second and third were no better. One stared so greedily at my breasts that I had to cut the interview short; the other might just as well have been one of the creeps who plagued women on the Paris streets, walking just steps behind while whispering obscenities in their ears.

Overnight, my dream city was turning into my personal nightmare. I had gravely underestimated what life would be like without the connection to a study program, without a landlady and her comfortable apartment, without friends to dine with and encourage me. Ada and my Swedish pals were long packed up and gone. Even the bar where we had been regulars had a new owner who looked at me with total indifference as he poured me *un calva*. It was hard to admit to myself, but I had been a complete fool to have blown all my money on a fantasy. There was no way I would find employment in the French film business as a foreigner. Goddard's *Breathless* would be the most expensive movie ticket I would ever purchase.

A fitting ending to my misadventure came with a trip to the south of France to track down an old boyfriend, Peter Tumarkin, as a favor to his parents who were deeply concerned that he hadn't contacted them since graduating from Harvard the year before. When last heard from, he claimed to be working as a farm laborer just ten kilometers north of Avignon. After an interminable bus trip, I was dropped off, suitcase in hand, at the property Peter had described in his letter and knocked on the farmhouse door. The lady of the house opened it, eyed me suspiciously while I rapidly introduced myself and explained that I was looking for *"un American qui s'appelle Pierre"* who I thought was working there. Madame nodded and grudgingly admitted that the young man in question was with her husband out in the fields, that I could wait on the porch for them to return at sunset.

By now, I desperately needed to use a bathroom and was directed to the outhouse. I didn't think that I had fastened the metal latch, but, when I was done, I couldn't open the door. As I panicked and kept tugging away at the latch, I couldn't help but be aware that my situation was a bad joke; could there be a better ending for my dream of becoming a film director in Paris than being trapped in a stinking outhouse? Growing ever more desperate, I finally called out for help in French, *"Au secours! Au secours!"* feeling stupid that, as I shouted, I was picturing Lillian Gish, the great silent film star tied to the railroad tracks calling, "Help! Help!" as a train engine rushed towards her while the villain twirled his mustache. Of course, Madame finally arrived, easily swinging open the door while regarding me with that sardonic smile only the French can muster. Peter, dressed in soiled overalls in imitation of his farmer boss, was pleased to see me but brushed off his parents' pleas to return home.

After that miserable experience, I was back in Manhattan within a week, dead broke after a final few days at the roulette tables in Monte Carlo. If it wasn't for the generosity of Amarjit's friends who offered up their couch for me to sleep on, I might have wound up sleeping on a bench in Central Park. With little choice but to push on or return to Cambridge with my tail drooping between my legs, I somehow summoned up my resolve to once more find a way into the film business even if I had to first detour into television. My first stops were CBS, NBC and ABC, the three major broadcast networks, since they were the only game in town, but when I told interviewers that I hoped to be hired as an assistant to a director of shows like *Playhouse 90* or *Kraft Mystery Theater* they stared as if I were from a galaxy far, far away and replied that if I learned stenography (the same old story), I could aim for a spot as secretary to one of their producers. Then if I was really lucky, *he* might even allow me to visit a set in his company. It was so infuriating. And disheartening. I then remembered that Al Capp, the creator of the popular comic strip, *Li'l Abner*, and an acquaintance of Amarjit's in Cambridge, might be able to help. When I called Al, he said he would be delighted to assist and suggested we meet at his East Side apartment. I was excited when I arrived. Al was famous, knew everybody in the world, and thinking, of him as a friend, I wasn't on my guard. He cordially invited me to sit on his couch, offered me a glass of wine and, faster than one of his cartoon characters could yell *Whaam*, his hands were all over my body as he tried to force his tongue into my mouth. I still remember the smell of his pomaded hair. I doubt I said good-bye as I fled.

After three months of feeling more and more wretched with each passing day, as each led to nowhere, I was just about ready to give up. I almost didn't knock on the door of the last person on my list, a Mr. Willard Van Dyke, praying he wouldn't regard me as just another tasty tidbit. To my delight, this gifted filmmaker (he had just been just been nominated for an Academy Award for his short documentary *Skyscraper)* was the complete opposite of Al Capp. Willard listened to my enthusiastic blathering about needing to make movies, then stopped me to write a letter on the spot introducing me to a documentary film group named Drew Associates. "They're a bunch of crazy people, and you'll fit right in." I did my best to look wildly happy while being sure, ingrate that I was, that in five minutes I would be tossing his introductory letter into the nearest trash can. I was quite sure that I wasn't interested in making documentaries; all I wanted was to be around people making feature movies with actors. But back out on the street, I knew that I might be blowing my last chance at entering, even if sideways, what was proving to be an unreachable world.

An hour later found me in a waiting room in a narrow building on West 43rd Street with no one in sight. Eventually a few people rushed through, and I was able to stop someone long enough to ask if I could meet the person named in Willard's letter, a Mr. D. A. Pennebaker. Finally, Mr. Pennebaker came out looking harried, and, in a rush of words, I quickly introduced myself with a fabricated story about accidentally losing the film I had just made that would show my nascent talent and how I would do anything to work at his company. I doubt he listened, but, not knowing how to dispose of me, he said, "Here, sit down and watch the film we just completed. It's special."

A screen dropped down, the lights were turned off, the projector on, and I was left alone to watch *Primary*, a documentary about the recent 1960 Kennedy/Humphrey primary fight in Wisconsin. To my untutored eyes, it seemed perfectly normal to follow behind Jack and Jackie as they charmed voters in club halls across the state, or climb as they climbed onto town hall stages to be greeted by adoring fans singing Kennedy's campaign song, "He's got high hopes, he's got high hopes, nineteen sixty's the year for his high hopes," and be a fly on the wall as the couple waited in a Milwaukee hotel room for the election returns to come in. Jack was trying his best to appear unflappable, and it was impossible not to be touched by Hubert Humphrey straight-talking to farmers but knowing that he hadn't a hope in hell against such radiant youth.

When the lights came back on, I felt bewildered. I didn't know why the film was "special," having seen only a few documentaries before, and with no language in which to frame my response. In the fiction films I'd seen, it seemed natural to move along with actors, but I had never thought about how that was accomplished. It was only after I was hired as an apprentice editor for fifty dollars a week that it became clear I had landed in the midst of a revolution in filmmaking. Until then, all documentary filmmakers were limited in what they could film by the weight of bulky cameras on tripods, linked by cable, to equally bulky sound recorders to keep them in perfect synchronization. The human eye could tell if they were even a fraction of second apart. Frustrated by this limitation, Pennebaker (known as "Penny" to his many friends), an engineer with the face of a young boy that would remain that way well into his nineties, along with cameraman Richard Leacock, a jaunty Englishman with an unconcealed taste for the ladies, had just built the first fully portable silent 16mm camera that could rest on their shoulders and be synchronized with a portable tape recorder without a connecting cable. It meant that they could follow a subject just about anywhere while the person holding the microphone and recorder could move just as freely.

Primary was the first film to be shot this way, and it was groundbreaking: a cameraperson could now capture "real life" without taking a hand in directing the action. The French labeled this new way of moviemaking cinema verité, the Americans called it Direct Cinema, and people have argued, in true French fashion ever since about whether there really is such a thing as "verité" since the cameraperson chooses what to record the moment a camera is turned on. Pennebaker and Leacock found a like-minded partner in Robert Drew, a journalist at *Time* magazine, who had persuaded his publishers to fund a company to produce this new form of documentaries with a promise from ABC to broadcast them, adding Albert and David Maysles of *Grey Gardens* and *Gimme Shelter* fame to the mix.

The New York streets never looked more beautiful to me than that first morning on the job when I carried a stack of metal film cans to DuArt Labs just a few blocks away for processing. I even liked the smell of the negatives inside them. It was hard to believe that it had been only three years since I had fled these very same streets, unable to see anything beyond my own blind panic. Though I had been born there, with a birth certificate to prove it, I had never really thought of myself as a bona fide New Yorker. *The City* was Manhattan, and, for a girl who grew up where Brooklyn meets the Atlantic Ocean, Manhattan was a jeweled island where only the rich and talented were destined to live. But on that rainy day, I felt that the City had thrown open its arms to me and I loved every minute of it.

The three other apprentices, beside myself, were all women, young and pretty. The atmosphere wasn't exactly like *Mad Men*, but we were fair game, and the running joke was that we had been hired so that the guys "could see our cute lil' asses hanging over the trim barrel" when we bent to retrieve the short film clips that had accidentally been dropped to its bottom by the editors. But not one of them made any crude advances towards us. In keeping with the time, there were glasses of wine at lunch and drinking after work in the lounge of the fabled Algonquin Hotel around the corner — my favorite, a Whiskey Alexander, which I thought immensely sophisticated — and we gossiped endlessly about our bosses, particularly about Drew who had a fierce temper and whom I saw yank a door off its hinges in one of his rages. It was more fun to gossip about Ricky Leacock, who had arrived one morning, typically pleased as punch with himself, and announcing in his plummy British accent, "I had a marvelous fuck last night!" as he patted his belly.

Until then, I had been studying, as best I could on my own, film lighting and camera angles, but I had never given much thought to film editing, and I was instantly drawn to the process, fascinated by how easily one could change the meaning of a scene by rearranging individual shots. Seeing my eagerness to even just touch the filmstrips he was working with, one of the editors offered to take me on as his apprentice. My first assignment was to prepare the new footage, the dailies, for editing by matching the magnetic sound track to the picture, a pairing that we take for granted in our digital age. It would have taken hours trying to figure out how to get them synchronized were it not for a simple solution invented at the beginning of talking pictures: an assistant on set would hold a small chalkboard called the clapstick in front of the lens with the camera roll number, scene and film title scrawled on it, then bang down a movable stick attached to the top. It was then up to an assistant editor to match that sharp "bang" sound with the film frame where the stick hit the board. I happily performed the job on a very noisy green Moviola, a machine that was invented in 1924 and was still the only editing console in use around the world. Since it could only handle one sound track at a time, the director would have to imagine how the main dialogue track played with the music and sound effects until the day they were all mixed together at a recording studio. I'm still in awe of the mixers who, like orchestra conductors, commanded the many reels of sounds in a back room with the flick of a switch and, with seeming magic, filtered out the interfering background noises.

A month later, Kennedy was elected president, and the office buzz was that, appreciative of *Primary*, he would grant special access to the Drew film team the day of his inauguration. Unsurprisingly, just a week before the event, that access was denied by the Secret Service. In a mad scramble, Drew decided that the company would still film Inauguration Day and follow three different people instead: Senator Hubert Humphrey, Scottie Lanahan (the only child of F. Scott Fitzgerald and Zelda), and John Steinbeck, author of the Pulitzer Prize-winning novel *The Grapes of Wrath*. Senator Humphrey was assigned to Leacock who, to my astonishment, asked me to be his "sound girl." I panicked since I had never been on a film shoot and knew absolutely nothing about how to record sound, but Ricky assured me that an hour's lesson with the new Nagra tape recorder would more than do.

All six of us arrived the day before the big event in fine January weather with our equipment and *Time* magazine press passes pinned to our lapels. I was flying so high with excitement I wouldn't have needed a plane to carry me there. Within hours, an unforeseen storm blanketed Washington, D.C. in snow, with eight inches falling by evening. As befitted a professional working girl, I was wearing a skirt, nylon stockings and low-heeled pumps. Every pair of boots in the city had sold out instantly. But still running on pure adrenaline, I didn't feel the cold slapping at my bare legs as Ricky and I took our places in the press stand opposite where the grandees of both parties were seated to watch the Parade of the States go by. All were celebrating the day, including the new states of Alaska and Hawaii, with high-stepping marching bands and floats packed with not always appropriately dressed young ladies.

I had put a wireless mike on Senator Humphrey and was privy to every comment he and his wife, Muriel, made to each other. After a short while, Muriel, though bundled up to her chin in furs to keep out the chill, began to murmur complaints as the parade dragged on. "Daddy, I'm so cold . . . Can't we go home?" to which the senator patiently replied, "No, Mommy, not until our state goes by." "But Minnesota may be another hour away," she moaned. Joe Kennedy was seated not far off in the front row, and when his son, the president-elect, rode by in his open limousine, the proud papa stood up and let out a savage whoop with such unabashed exultation that I felt I was witnessing something not meant to be seen by strangers. Senator Humphrey, ever the gentleman in spite of his primary losses, said to no one in particular, "My, oh my . . . Mr. and Mrs. Kennedy must be awfully proud of their boy today."

By the time we got to the jammed Mall for the swearing-in ceremony, we could barely make out the main figures on the platform as our new president's thrilling words rang through the air: "And so, my fellow Americans: ask not what your country can do for you — ask what you can do for your country." It was the first day of *Camelot,* and Robert Frost, the first poet ever invited to speak at a presidential inauguration, recited his poetry as the wind played havoc with his famous white hair. To complete the extraordinary day, Ricky and I talked our way into one of the many inaugural balls and, high on champagne, danced what remained of the night away. When we returned to New York, I was excited to be bumped up to assistant editor and, with an increase in salary, was able to bid farewell to my friends' couch and rent an apartment with two other women in Yorkville on the Upper East Side, home to delicious German bakeries. But not before rushing down to a Macy's rug sale with my first overtime pay in my pocket and buying a handwoven Persian rug for five hundred dollars that I have on my living room floor to this day.

four

As happy as I was with my job and living in Manhattan, my heart remained in Boston with Amarjit, and I couldn't imagine my life without him. But after two years of weekend commuting — thanks to the new Eastern Airlines Shuttle where, for thirteen dollars one way, you simply lined up at the gate, no reservation needed, and boarded the next plane out — the strain on both of us was taking its toll. After much indecision we finally decided to get married. With some trepidation, I told my parents about our plans, and, as I feared, they were not only shocked but absolutely opposed. They had known that I was seeing someone from India but hadn't taken it very seriously. I realized too late that I should have first brought Amarjit home to meet them, as I was sure he would have instantly won them over. Accusing them of racism, I declared that I would go ahead even without their approval, but the frost lasted for only a month since we found it impossible to remain angry at one another for long.

What finally brought them around, I think, was that Amarjit was not a *goy*, meaning he was neither Catholic nor Protestant but a non-practicing Hindu. They were also touched that he had never known his father, a doctor who had served in the British Navy and whose ship was torpedoed during World War II. As an only son, he was raised with the image of a heroic father, forever absent, and a devoted mother who never remarried. Jai and her young son had to flee their ancestral home in Lahore after India was partitioned in 1948 and the city became part of Pakistan, leaving them forever traumatized by the terror of that forced departure in the middle of the night, rioting mobs on the streets and the nightmarish train ride south. More than fifteen million people were uprooted in a few months, and, as the great migration drew to its end, nearly two million people were counted as dead. It was a story my parents readily identified with as so many of their relatives had had to flee their homes in Russia or died in concentration camps during World War II.

More fortunate than most of their fellow Indians, both Hindu and Muslim, Mrs. Chopra's parents had landholdings north of New Delhi where they were able to restart their lives. Jai continued her studies and was the first woman in India to receive an advanced university degree in mathematics. It was there that she met Maria Montessori and, inspired by her teaching, settled in the city of Patiala, close to her extended family, and opened a Montessori school of her own. Starting with preschoolers, she added grades and trained teachers as the students progressed until, by the time I met her, they'd had eighth-grade classes for many years. When she learned that her son was going to marry an American woman, she put on her best face and made plans for her first trip to the States.

When my parents finally met Amarjit, they were relieved that he seemed so "American," and, in a complete about-face, they went all out for a big wedding and reserved the penthouse ballroom at the old St. George Hotel in Brooklyn Heights, which had floor-to-ceiling windows that looked across the harbor to the glittering towers of Manhattan. With one of Amarjit's cousins as best man and one of my New York roommates as best woman, we were married in a civil ceremony in a judge's chambers. I was so nervous I could barely stop my head from shaking. The next evening, in full wedding dress regalia, with something borrowed and something blue, we were driven to the grand event in style. My father's many sisters instantly fell in love with the princely Amarjit and vied with each other to dance with him. Amarjit's favorite uncle from New Delhi accompanied his mother, and, most importantly, his wealthy paternal uncle, who lived on Lake Geneva with his English wife, deigned to come and give his blessings.

With the stroke of a pen, I was now officially Mrs. Amarjit Chopra. It was 1963 and a time when women rarely questioned changing their family name to that of their husband's, and I was no exception. With Amarjit's blessing, I continued my split life as Mrs. Chopra, flying back to our Cambridge apartment to be with him every weekend. Having fully embraced living in the States, Amarjit was reluctant to visit India where relatives were eager to meet his American bride. But he finally had to give into his mother's pleas, along with my ready assent as I was more than eager to see the world that had shaped him.

From the moment we landed at the airport in New Delhi I was surrounded by women smiling at me and piling wreaths of colorful flowers around my neck while bangles were forced over my wrists. Smiling back at everyone, we made our way to Mrs. Chopra's sedan and were driven by her chauffeur through the city where I was dazzled by the riot of colors and aromas streaming through our windows, the sound of the vendors hawking their wares, and the stray cows ambling down the street. I was longing for one of my Camel cigarettes, but I didn't dare smoke, and for the entire three-week visit I had to sneak outside like a naughty kid to take a few puffs and hide the evidence.

The house, when we finally arrived, was a pleasant modern dwelling with a room reserved for Mrs. Chopra's beloved only son. "The Duchess," as she was teasingly referred to by close family, had four servants in addition to the chauffeur — a cook, a sweeper, a laundry woman and a maid of all work. As Amarjit explained to me when he saw the shocked look on my face, their employment was more for their sake than for hers since the wages they received supported their large extended families, his mother paying extra for their dentists and doctors.

We awoke our first morning to the sound of a servant carrying tea and rolls to our bedside. From that moment on, we were never left alone or allowed to do anything for ourselves. If I went to pick up even a tissue, a servant rushed to my side to do it for me. For the next twenty days, every lunch and dinner was booked with relatives who wanted to honor the "foreign-returned" Amarjit and his bride. It was a kind of *Groundhog Day,* except instead of repeating the same day, we repeated the same meal ritual in different homes. We would enter the dining room with its chairs placed against all four walls, the men seated on one side, the women on the other, while in the center gleamed a long table heaped with North Indian foods of every sort. Everything was delicious, but I could barely taste it since all eyes were on me as I took a first bite. I would nod my head to express delight, and, when that ordeal was over and all the women satisfied, the men would chuckle and sneak out to have their glasses of Johnny Walker Red, illegal and therefore much prized. And I would manage to sneak out for my cigarette while Amarjit covered for me.

As much as we both tried, Jit's mother and I were unable to strike up any real friendship. Although unfailingly polite, I knew that she longed for her son to permanently return to India; now that he was married to an American, the chances of that happening were even slimmer. On one of those rare afternoons when we weren't visiting relatives, I hoped to please her by learning to cook a curry under her direction, taking notes like a good wife while her cook surreptitiously corrected the amount of spices her mistress was adding to the tikka masala. My yearning to break free to travel on our own was increasing daily, but, save for one visit to the massive Red Fort in Delhi, the main residence of the emperors of the Mughal dynasty and the site of a massive uprising against British rule, it was not to be. I can still feel the relief that washed through me when we boarded the airplane at departure.

Back in the States, I continued to edit at Drew Associates. Sitting in the editor's seat was a perfect way to learn how a documentary movie is put together: without the responsibility of deciding how and what to shoot, while free to curse the now absent cameraman for failing to film the most important moment. While trying to figure out how to cut such a scene one rainy morning, I was told I had better "pick up a call on line 2 from a crying female." To my surprise, it was my old partner, Paula Kelley, sobbing her heart out. "They've taken over. The bastards have taken over. They've voted me off the board." "Hold on a minute . . . What are you talking about?" It took me a few seconds to understand that the "they" she was referring to were the Club 47's board members.

It appeared that our decision, five years earlier, to turn the club into a nonprofit had caused her present grief. Though we had formed a board consisting of the two of us and a few close friends, we had never bothered to convene the required meetings. If the IRS had uncovered our negligent behavior, our educational status would have been in jeopardy. When Paula became the sole manager, her lawyer chastised her about our dereliction of duty, and she immediately mended her ways. In time, our friends left the board to move to other cities, and she replaced them with folksingers dedicated to what had become their cherished performance space. It proved to be Paula's fatal mistake. The recast board voted to remove her. It had happened just the night before, and she was still in shock.

I could barely fathom the cruelty. It was one thing for the musicians to treat Paula with thinly veiled disdain for being "management," but to unceremoniously kick one of the founders out the door was beyond my imagination. Distressed, I promised to get to Cambridge by evening and force our way into the club if necessary to reclaim it. In spite of the now heavy rainfall, I did manage to arrive around 9PM. The club was in darkness, with one lone figure hovering in the doorway. It was Paula, with a useless key in her hand. The board had changed the lock. If I had been puzzled before, it took less than a second for me to become incensed when I tried the old key myself. With no enemy in sight to challenge or a brick in hand to smash the windows, we had to admit defeat. The terrible evening ended with a dazed Paula slowly drifting down Mt. Auburn Street in a cloud of bitterness.

I wasn't entirely sorry to hear that the club closed forever in less than a year. Although it was more popular than ever, it couldn't sell enough coffee to keep its creditors at bay. When I happened to pass by that same door in 2008, my eye caught sight of a blue oval plaque on the building's exterior, just like the ones I'd seen in London marking the homes of England's great inventors and artists. Put there by the Cambridge Historical Commission, it bore the legend: "Here Joan Baez and Bob Dylan sang duets, Muddy Waters played the blues," going on to name other famous singers who "led the '60s folk revival." I probably grinned from ear to ear as I tried to absorb the words and took a few photos on my phone to look at later. I wanted to e-mail one to Paula, but try, as I might, I have never been able to locate her. It's as though she disappeared not only down Mt. Auburn Street but also off the face of the earth.

Seemingly overnight, Bob Drew lost his *Time* backing and was forced to shut down. It happened so fast I could barely comprehend that my wonderful job on West 43rd Street would no longer exist and that I would have to give up that New York City life that I so loved, as there were no comparable jobs to be had there. The landscape for women in film hadn't changed at all. Amarjit and I found ourselves, really for the first time, living the life of a married couple, and I tried settling into domesticity, doing my best to be a good wife by getting up early to prepare his breakfast and improve my chicken curries. It helped that I had been absorbed into his circle of high-spirited friends who got together every weekend to play poker or, if the weather was warm, go sailing off the North Shore. It reminded me of happy nights with my Swedish painters minus the Calvados, although we did consume large quantities of wine. Amarjit, a great storyteller, broke his toe while telling a tall tale, and as soon as we docked I drove him to the hospital where, I like to joke, they proceeded to take out his appendix and left the toe untouched (he had spoken of pain in his abdomen while the on-call physician was examining him).

When his group of pals expanded to include some young architects who were eager to stage a "happening," the '60s forerunner to performance art, we rented an empty warehouse on one of the derelict Boston piers and got busy clearing the junk from a few floors to prepare for a black-tie dance party for five hundred people: admission five dollars a head, one drink included. It was Club 47 on a mega scale. My job was to provide the music and be one of the miniskirted go-go dancers on a raised platform with colored spotlights beaming down as we writhed to the sounds of Elvis and Buddy Holly while Jit rotated as one of the bartenders.

The event was a grand success, lasting until dawn, but so exhausting to produce that I started to look for a less extravagant way for us to enjoy ourselves. I stumbled on an ad in the *Boston Globe* for an old farmhouse with four bedrooms, a waterfall, and a swimmable pond, all just a few hours away in Connecticut. By pooling our money, we rented it for the summer and wound up spending most weekends down there, drinking and cooking and playing the inevitable poker games in no particular order. A few of us even tried our hands at growing vegetables, and, though I had never touched the earth before except to fall down on it, I began to develop a real passion for gardening, thrilled to reach into the earth and pull out a handful of new potatoes or twist off a sugar snap pea from a vine.

But as much as I loved the fellowship, I just couldn't just sit back and be idle in spite of having a husband who could support me. My mother would occasionally telephone to ask when Amarjit and I would be having a baby and would teasingly sigh that she would never become a grandmother like all of her friends, but having a baby was the last thing on my mind. I still badly wanted to find a film job, and, if it could be close to home, all the better. I was beginning to worry that Amarjit's and my own commitment to each other would be in danger of slipping if I returned to a weekend commute. A chance to make a feature flickered bright when we both became entranced with a witty crime novel set in 1930s Paris, and, with his ability to pay for an option if it wasn't too expensive, I tried obtaining the film rights. I never even received a reply from the book's agent. It was probably just as well since I was too inexperienced to know that a period movie was the most expensive kind to produce, with its costumes and period cars. It was depressing to admit that fiction filmmaking was still very far out of my reach. As for documentaries, the Boston/Cambridge area, though not exactly a backwater, produced only a few that were largely financed through Harvard's Peabody Museum of Archaeology.

Knowing that I had to find work even if it was far from ideal, I took a chance and approached Robert Gardner, who had set up the Film Study Center next to the Peabody with the hope that he might be seeking an editor. A great-grandson of Isabella Stuart Gardner, Bob had inherited Isabella's taste for adventure but, instead of collecting paintings and tapestries for her eponymous museum in Boston, he had organized an expedition to the central highlands of Papua New Guinea to produce a documentary about the Dani people and their elaborate system of warfare. Without benefit of Pennebaker's equipment, he had filmed the warriors as it had been done for decades — shooting first and recording wild, unsynchronized sound later. He agreed to hire me to make it appear like all these separate parts belonged together. I found the work rather tedious as it was a repeat of my very first assignment at Drew Associates when, tucked away in a corner editing room, I spent hours trying to match ear-splitting sounds to the race cars zooming around the track at the Indy 500.

I wasn't very drawn to Bob's style of filmmaking, which, though gorgeous to look at, seemed too staged to my cinema verité trained eyes, but I was very drawn to Bob, which upset me. Amarjit and I had been married for less than two years, and I was already restless without our friends to fill the air around us. My boss was tall and handsome, and I had come to realize that his cool exterior hid a rather shy person. It didn't take long for the two of us to become secret lovers, shutting the door to his office on many a late afternoon. Whether Amarjit or Bob's wife were aware of it I'll never know, but I do know Bob was divorced soon after. By then, with my work on his film done, he and I had drifted apart.

I barely had time to worry about what to do next when I heard Ricky Leacock's voice on the phone asking, "Are you ready to make a film in South Dakota? The town is Aberdeen, and, God knows, I have no idea where it is," his words reverberating like "Ode to Joy" in my ears. Shortly after the collapse of Drew Associates, he and Pennebaker decided to team up, with their first paying assignment coming from the *Saturday Evening Post*. Just a week before, quintuplets, the first to survive in the States, had been born to Mary Ann and Andrew Fischer of Aberdeen, South Dakota, and like the Dionne Quints in Canada before them, the Fischer Quints became an overnight sensation, with every newspaper in the country headlining the story. Ricky agreed to be the one to take on the job of producing a television special that the *Post* hoped would triple the impact of their exclusive magazine stories and was asking me to be his sound recordist. Our assignment would be to make a documentary that celebrated the near-miraculous births.

I was thrilled by the offer but conflicted; my short affair with Bob, which I had kept secret from Amarjit, had forced me to admit to myself that our marriage was on shaky grounds. If I left now for a few months, there was no way of knowing how much further damage my absence would do. When I told Jit about Ricky's call, instead of asking that I stay home with him, he was happy for me, generously adding that it "promised to be a great learning experience." That was all I needed to hear to put aside any doubts. A week later, with a much-less-burdened heart and with assorted microphones in a travel bag and a Nagra over my shoulder, I was on a plane with Ricky to a part of America that was to prove more foreign to me than India. As I stepped off the plane, all I could see was flat prairie stretching out forever in all four directions. Having spent years amidst the hills and curving roads of New England, I found the unchanging landscape unsettling, with no surprises around a corner. A taxi drove us straight to the hospital where, with a sense of wonder, we both gazed down at Mary Margaret, Mary Magdalene, Mary Ann, Mary Catherine and their brother, James Andrew, each alone in their own isolette and so small that I could have held any one of them in the palm of my hand.

Out at the Fischer family farm the next morning, Mr. Fischer greeted us with a friendly welcome, but it was clear that Mrs. Fischer was not overly pleased to see us. She could see that she and her family were about to be caught up in a frenzy of commercial activity that would only get worse; and she had little choice but to accept the *Post's* money as she and her husband were struggling to raise the five kids they already had on Andrew's grocery store clerk paycheck. Their front yard was already a beehive of activity under the direction of the *Post's* still photographer, who had arrived before us and was busy shouting to his crew from the top of a tall ladder to bunch together the gifts pouring in from Aberdeen's shopkeepers to maximize the effect of what was already a spectacular array of baby clothes, baby shoes, baby diapers, baby food, baby blankets, a new washer and dryer, a truckload of milk, two large refrigerators and, to top it all off, two shiny new automobiles.

This contrived staging of the Fischers' lives was so irresistible to us that Ricky and I immediately unpacked our gear and began filming. This was our first big mistake: we gave in to the temptation to film the reality before our eyes, the "behind the scenes," rather than sticking to our assignment, especially when the *Post* photographer asked the exhausted family to pretend to be driving on a country road in Andy's prized Model T Ford while circling round and round a tree in their front yard to get his perfect shot. When it appeared in the *Post* within a week, Andy and the five kids looked appropriately happy, but MaryAnn looks in a state of shock.

We also couldn't resist filming the chamber of commerce meetings where members were busy making plans to accommodate the horde of visitors they expected would be coming to Aberdeen and, while there, shopping at their stores. You could tell they were already hearing the sweet sound of millions of coins *ka-ching*-ing into their open cash registers, and we were especially intrigued by the moral conundrum members were only now beginning to face: how to accommodate this money-paying crowd who would expect to see the babies without the board members feeling guilty about the intrusion? They couldn't but recall the heartless way the Dionne Quints had been treated some thirty years before when the Canadian government adopted the five baby girls shortly after their birth and made a fortune in ticket sales when they moved the infants to a compound that allowed tourists to observe them from behind one-way screens. These viewings went on for almost seven years until public outrage at last put a stop to it all.

With no easy way around the problem, the chamber members asked Mary Ann and Andrew if they would permit just two Quint viewings a day, excluding Sundays. They thought it a reasonable request. Andrew at first seemed amenable to the idea, but Mary Ann fiercely put her foot down when I asked during an interview, "Do you agree with your husband?" "They are never going to be on display as far as I am concerned. Never!" I visibly winced. Weren't Ricky and I doing the same thing as all the other reporters: accepting pay to exploit their situation even if we were actually filming them being exploited? It only made it worse that Mary Ann had been willing to do the filmed interview with us because I was a sympathetic female.

The chamber of commerce members reluctantly let go their dreams of dollar bills raining down from heaven and settled for a banquet at which the town notables honored the couple with lavish praise and song. Mary Ann could barely keep a straight face as the soprano soloist went off key, and I had to put a hand to my mouth to stop my own laughter from being heard. The town's residents found the best spots on the sidewalks to watch the big parade on Main Street, laughing at the sight of grown-ups, dressed as babies, bouncing atop one of the floats. Even the Aberdeen High School marching band got into the act, with their baton twirler getting a chance to strut her stuff. In the middle of it all, Mary Ann and Andrew smiled and waved to the crowd lining the streets from an open convertible, just like Buzz Aldrin and Neil Armstrong would do four years later when they returned from the moon.

I once again started commuting down to Manhattan to edit in the Leacock Pennebaker offices. Although I had learned the mechanics of editing and was permitted to cut individual scenes while working as an assistant editor at Drew Associates, this was my first attempt at shaping an entire film. Strange to say, there was no one person who taught me this craft; I somehow instinctively understood the process from day one. But, to my great disappointment, when we delivered *A Happy Mother's Day* to the *Post*, the magazine took our footage and edited their own version for ABC TV as ours was so clearly about the commercialization of the family. It was painful to see our work tossed aside, but none of this really came as a surprise. Although I had foolishly hoped that the magazine would be dazzled by our film and broadcast it as is, not too deep down I knew that we had produced a film that was the opposite of what they had paid for. For some time, the quints' birthday photos appeared annually on the magazine's cover until artificial means of ensuring multiple births ended it all. Although my name shared credit with Ricky on the film since I had actively partnered with him and done most of the editing, it was excluded in the Leacock / Pennebaker advertising. I hadn't seen it coming, and it hurt deeply, especially after such a close collaboration. It was only years later, after I gained some notice for my first feature film ,that my name suddenly appeared, but, grateful for the chances they had given me, I had forgiven them long before.

five

I T W A S A big letdown to be back in Cambridge after being so engaged with the Fischer Quints film, and I was once again afflicted with shpilkes, that wonderful Yiddish phrase denoting "ants in your pants." I was trying almost desperately to find a subject of my own to film when one fell into my lap. My oldest cousin, Phyllis, Aunt Bella "the Boss's" daughter, was now living in Los Angeles and was married to a hotshot Hollywood agent. Harold phoned me one day with a hot tip just after the Beatles made their first appearance on *The Ed Sullivan Show*. "You can make a fortune if you can get behind the scenes with your camera and film a new group that is going to be even bigger than the Beatles." He was talking about The Wild Ones, five young guys from Brooklyn who had just landed a job as the house band at the newly opened nightclub, Arthur, on Manhattan's Upper East Side. The owner, Sybil Burton, was receiving intense media coverage due to Richard Burton's divorcing her to marry his Cleopatra, Elizabeth Taylor, and Arthur was overflowing with celebrities. Within weeks of the band playing there, Sybil had married one of the singers, Jordan Christopher.

With equipment borrowed from Leacock Pennebaker and my friend Peter Powell volunteering as cameraman, I was all set to make my fortune. Harold introduced me to Sybil, who cheerily gave me the go-ahead, even agreeing to appear in the film. Her publicists and agents were sure that they had a hot property on their hands, and The Wild Ones certainly looked great on stage. They already had a record deal with United Artists, and the more-than-competent Danny Secunda and Teddy Randazzo were hired to arrange and produce the album. When the pair arrived at the nightclub to listen to the band's music for the first time, my heart sank. I realized that I was filming a mass delusion. The band didn't have one original song to play, and it was going to be up to Randazzo to come up with the tunes pretty quickly. I should have known enough to walk away but was intrigued by the absurdity of the situation, not unlike how Ricky and I felt filming the exploitation of the Fischer family. Most likely, I was simply hooked on the excitement of finally making a movie of my own.

But as hard as Randazzo tried, not one new song materialized, and it became clear that The Wild Ones' first album would have to consist entirely of cover songs. While Randazzo was working overtime on their behalf, the band members were having the time of their lives. Only weeks before, these kids had been waiters working for tips, and they were now spending their days fantasizing about the worldwide fame Sybil's publicists predicted was coming their way. Each scene I filmed with them had me shaking my head in disbelief. Eddie, one of the twenty-one-year-old vocalists told me with all due modesty as he looked straight into the camera, "It's taken a long time for the world to discover me." Jordan Christopher had already made his leap into the easy life the day he married Sybil and moved into her Central Park West apartment, settling into the back seat of her chauffeured limousine as though he was to the manor born.

Just days after the album was released as *The Arthur Sound Recorded Live at Arthur,* with a Richard Avedon photo of the young men holding Sybil aloft on its cover, United Artists was forced to withdraw it. The buying public had caught on that the "Live at Arthur" part was a lie; friends at the recording studio had been instructed when to clap and whistle. Then, when Sybil saw a copy of the edited film, she sent me a message with just a few words: "If you ever show the movie I will sue you." I was crushed but not surprised. If only I had heeded Sam Goldwyn's warning, "A verbal contract isn't worth the paper it's written on." Too inexperienced to ask Sybil to put her signature on a release form, I had taken her at her word.

With my batting average as a director now zero — *Wild Ones* and *A Happy Mother's Day* both unreleased — I went into a funk and, for the first time since I set out on my solo journey to Paris, questioned why I had ever thought I could get anywhere in the film business. I had tried New York and Boston, and Hollywood's doors hadn't remotely cracked open for women as far as I could tell. But life is full of unintended consequences, most often unpleasant ones, but in this case it was the total opposite: a phone call from the secretary to David Picker, the head of feature film production at United Artists, telling me that Mr. Picker had screened *Wild Ones*, thought it great and wanted to meet me at his New York office. It seemed that Sybil had inadvertently done me a huge favor by sending over her copy of the film, hoping Mr. Picker would cast her new husband in one of his movies. Picker's compliment was beyond thrilling.

With my body tense with fear, I rode up the crowded elevator in the UA building on Seventh Avenue and barely managed to calm down as I sent in my name at reception. David greeted me warmly and immediately asked why I was "wasting my talents doing documentaries" when I should be making features. I eagerly replied that a feature was exactly what I had wanted to do but I'd lost hope and, "I'm not sure where to begin now." "Write a screenplay." "I never have," I responded. "Then find a writer who can, and bring me the script." He made it all sound so simple.

When I boarded the flight to Boston on the Eastern Shuttle I found an empty seat next to Amarjit's Turkish pal, Egon Ali-Oglu, and began to tell him about what had just happened to me. I thought he wasn't hearing a word of my excited babbling, seemingly more absorbed in leafing through *Time* magazine than in listening, but when I said "I have to find a screenwriter," he pointed to an article in the magazine. "What about this guy?" It was a glowing review of *An End to Chivalry*, a novella and five short stories written by his friend, Tom Cole. "You two would really like each other. I'll call and arrange a brunch so you can meet. He lives in Boston." True to his word, Egon did call Tom's home the next day, and his wife, Ellen, answered. When asked if she thought that Tom might be interested in meeting a director who wanted to collaborate on a screenplay, she answered that, although her husband had never written one, he loved movies and was sure that he would be delighted. As soon as Egon relayed the news, I rushed out to purchase Tom's book, praying I would like it since we were heading towards a sort of blind date. My wish came true. I loved the stories. Egon was a wonderful cook, and it was arranged that all I had to do was show up for a brunch that Sunday at my very own apartment.

The meeting ran into trouble even before it began. I had played poker with friends, drunk too much wine and stayed up most of the night before. When Tom and Ellen arrived, I was bleary-eyed and barely able to take part in the conversation, painfully aware that I had stupidly sabotaged my chance to impress a potential collaborator. Fortunately, Amarjit was clearheaded, and he and Tom took an immediate liking to each other and talked away, carrying us through the uneasy situation. Egon's food was much appreciated, but I barely ate any of it, wishing everyone would just go away and let me get back into bed. Tom politely asked if it was possible for him to see *Wild Ones*. I had already developed an aversion to the film and barely looked as we projected it on a fold-up screen. Tom was impressed and asked if we could get together soon since he was leaving in a few weeks for the MacDowell Colony, an artists' retreat in New Hampshire, to work on his novel.

When he arrived a few days later, Amarjit was at work, and I no longer had a hangover. It was only then that I realized how blind I had been at that brunch, not just to Tom's pleasing manners; his lively way of thinking was just the tip of what I found so appealing about him. We each threw out some ideas for possible scenarios and agreed to meet one more time before he left for the month. That one more time found us, once again, alone in my living room, with me perched on a window seat as Tom paced around the room, both of us pretending to be thinking about our possible script, aware of how intensely attracted we were to each other. My desire to embrace him shocked me as another affair was the last thing I was looking for. Even more shocking, I knew in that instant he was the man I was going to be with forever. With the Beatles singing *Michelle, Ma Belle* on the record player, I met him halfway across the room as though a magnet had drawn me to him. I know that he opened his jacket to welcome me and I slipped my arms around his slim waist as he gently kissed me.

Far more romantic than a motel, the MacDowell Colony, deep in the woods near Peterborough, New Hampshire, is perfectly set up for a lovers' tryst, especially on a snowy winter's day. The Colony, the oldest in the States, was from its beginning in 1908 an experiment with no precedent, providing time and space to artists across all disciplines, including Thornton Wilder who wrote *Our Town* while in residence, James Baldwin, Meredith Monk and Ta-Nehisi Coates. It's composed of individual wood cabins, some with pianos, where painters, writers and composers can work in absolute quiet, with lunch left in picnic baskets at their doors by staff wearing felt slippers over their shoes so as not to disturb. Tom greeted me in the main building where the residents dined in the evening, introduced me as a film director he was working with, and suggested I might enjoy visiting the town first. All very smoothly done.

An hour later I was lying in a state of bliss on the narrow bed in his writer's cabin, his arms around me, my head resting on his chest as though I'd always been there. We didn't become lovers that day or talk much, and, when we did, it was to make a plan — when I got home that evening, I would tell Amarjit that I had fallen in love with Tom Cole and wanted a divorce, and when he went back to Ellen the following week, he would ask for the same. This after meeting just a few times, knowing very little about each other but sure that we had to spend the rest of our lives together. On my drive home along New Hampshire's backcountry roads, I had a high as though I had been smoking weed, imagining that the glittering icicles hanging from the pine trees were a harbinger of the enriched life that lay ahead with Tom; his interests were so wide, his knowledge so deep. When I got home, Amarjit had a dinner waiting and was as kind as ever. My resolve to tell him about Tom and ask for a divorce instantly crumbled. And so it went for the entire week until my time at MacDowell began to seem like a dream.

Then early one evening, while Amarjit and I were both reading in the living room, the phone rang. It was Tom. "Did you tell him?" "No, I didn't . . . ," I whispered. "Well, I just told Ellen . . . . I'll be waiting for you at the Kirkland Inn tonight." Not too surprisingly, Amarjit took the news very calmly and was so gentlemanly that I wavered (it was only years later that I learned that he had been having an affair with a mutual friend). We even went out for a most cordial dinner at Chez Dreyfus during which he said that he understood that two artists would naturally want to be together. We ended the evening with his dropping me off at the inn and wishing me the best.

When I entered Tom's room, I hardly recognized him. He appeared to have collapsed in on himself, his whole body bathed in sweat. He managed to tell me that the scene at his apartment had been traumatic, especially for Ellen, who had begged him on her knees not to leave her, that our dream of getting together was idiotic, that we had to swear never to see each other again. Far from protesting, I could hardly wait to flee this man who now appeared a frightening stranger. I went back home to pick up my pleasant life with Amarjit and he calmly took me back. But the calmness was only a facade. We both knew that it was only a matter of time before we would divorce.

With no job and too disheartened to seek another writer to collaborate with, I was relieved when a job at the local public television station, WGBH, opened up for a director of live news broadcasts, and, without thinking through whether it was a good fit, I grabbed it. Hiring me was a daring move on their part. I would be the only female they had ever hired for the position, but in truth my first assignment wasn't very difficult. I would be directing the theater critic Elliot Norton's two-camera show, which had a substantial audience at a time when Boston was a major pre-Broadway tryout town and Elliot's criticisms were taken seriously by producers and directors like Mike Nichols and Neil Simon. Still, it was a novelty to sit in the control booth facing a bank of monitors, think fast and snap my fingers for "camera one" to be on air and then snap my fingers (faster than speaking the order) for a technician to switch over to "camera two," the close-up camera.

It didn't take long, though, to admit that taking the job had been a mistake. I couldn't picture myself spending the rest of my life inside a dark studio, especially with a supervisor, however civil, who assigned my week's work every Monday morning as though I was a cog in a wheel. Perhaps foolishly, I quit in less than a year. Had I stayed on, I could have had a good career in live television and led a very stable sort of existence with a decent monthly salary to boot. Even at twenty-eight, apparently I still possessed that blind faith of youth that a more fulfilling sort of work still lay in my future.

But any future plans I might have conceived were thrown into disarray when a slim book arrived in the mail, a gift from Tom of Isaac Babel's *Odessa Stories* that he knew I would enjoy. Holding it in my hands, knowing that he had touched its pages, my desire for him instantly came rushing back. I could think of little else. We began to meet in secret. Tom had the key to an apartment owned by his close friend and editor at the *Atlantic*, Billy Abrahams, so he could check on it when Billy was away. The setting was out of a melodrama, with drawn shades and furniture draped in white sheets. There were occasional motel trysts outside the city, and when both of us had reason to be in New York, we would rent a room for the afternoon at the Warwick or some other reasonably priced hotel. But these were mostly miserable occasions with very little joy in our sex, often ending with tears.

This went on for the better part of the year until we finally did manage to stop, during which time I began to actively pursue job leads in New York. I remain completely blank about the circumstances that brought me to the CBS offices of Burt Benjamin, the executive producer of some of the most successful news programs in prime-time television, to inquire about a directing job. It's possible that someone at WGBH heard about an opening and wrote a letter of recommendation on my behalf. If not that, I now wonder how in the world I had the audacity to even inquire when not a single female had been hired to write, let alone direct one of his shows. But hired I was to direct the first in a series for the new CBS program, *The Twenty-First Century with Walter Cronkite*.

I've been asked what motivated Burt Benjamin to hire a female, and it still puzzles me. It couldn't have been the emergence of the women's liberation movement of the early 1970s as it was still three or four years in the future. It may simply have been that, to Benjamin's eyes, this particular episode, *The Home of the Future*, was eminently suitable for a woman to helm, and I happened to walk through the door. It certainly was bold, especially if you picture a world where only three networks control all the news and entertainment we receive — no cable channels, no internet — with the white men who anchor the nightly news broadcasts appearing like gods to us. Walter Cronkite, called "the most trusted man in America," reigned supreme among them. He had been the one to announce Kennedy's assassination to the world just three years before, something I will always remember as I stood in shock in a beauty salon with hair dripping from an interrupted shampoo.

Not surprisingly, only men were hired to direct the rest of the series, which didn't upset me since they were a far cry from the cinema verité films that I had come to appreciate and hoped to continue with on my own. Shots were cut to illustrate Cronkite's narration so there wasn't a single scene in the finished episode that unfolded naturally on its own. I still retain fond memories of flying to Carbondale, Illinois, for a segment with the visionary architect, Buckminster Fuller, in his geodesic dome and watching Mr. Cronkite drop down from the sky in a helicopter, land on Bucky's lawn minutes before the interview whose lighting I had prepared, and rise up immediately after the interview was over, leaving me to do the filming of the famous dome, which I assumed Mr. Cronkite would describe from the comfort of a recording studio as though he had been there to see it all. I was therefore greatly disappointed when Amarjit and I sat down to watch the show the night it aired (in typical network fashion, I hadn't been part of the editing) and neither Bucky or his dome were included. Instead Burt Benjamin had used the interview I shot with the world famous architect, Philip Johnson, but, for some unfathomable reason, he didn't include the location we filmed at, Johnson's iconic Glass House that is now part of the National Trust.

On my return, Amarjit and I finally decided to call it quits and seek a Mexican divorce, now being recognized in the States, a quick procedure that required only one partner to be present. I was grateful when he volunteered to be the one to fly down to Juarez and happily volunteered to move out while he was away, eager for a place with no associations to our failed marriage. Taking with me only the four ladder-back chairs that I had found and restored when Paula and I cleared out Fournier's junk shop, I rented a small studio apartment nearby, hoping for I didn't know what.

It was then that my anxiety attacks returned, becoming so intense that I became afraid to leave my apartment without a bottle of Valium in my pocket. As before, I felt ashamed and didn't tell a soul, keeping it my own dark secret. I was still madly in love with Tom, but, as yet another year dragged on, I had less and less hope of his ever leaving his marriage. He occasionally wrote to me, rarely telephoned. When my phone rang one morning and it was Tom asking if I could join him for lunch, I almost didn't go, knowing it would leave me even more miserable. When I arrived, he was there waiting for me. Without any preamble, he took my hand in his and told me that he had left Ellen weeks ago and rented an apartment on the Charles River, near MIT, where he was now teaching in the literature department. I was so dumbfounded that I couldn't speak. "Show me your lease," I finally blurted out. Without replying, he bade me stand up and steered me out the restaurant door to his parked car and pulled the all-important document from his glove compartment. I was by now so overflowing with joy that I covered his face with kisses.

Being in psychoanalysis for three years had saved Tom's inner life. When I finally confessed to him my dark secret, he assured me that anxiety was a fairly common malady. I had never met anyone in therapy before and knew very little about it. With his help, I found a doctor I could talk to, and talk I did, but not before the doctor insisted that I toss away my bottle of tranquilizers. Those four-times-a-week sessions were the best education I ever had. In traditional Freudian style, I lay on a couch while he sat behind me and to the side. He rarely spoke, so it was a shock when he said in his soft, southern-accented voice, "You prefer to have these anxiety attacks than let the anger you're feeling rise to the surface." I was so outraged at what I thought was an accusation that I sat up and turned to look at him and sputtered, "You're the crazy one, I'd rather kill myself than have another one." But once I calmed down a bit, we began a series of detective games in which I tried to pinpoint the moment when I began to feel anxious, then reconstruct what I had been doing or who I might have been with. A pattern emerged that proved the doctor right. It took quite a few months to get good at warding off the attacks by recognizing that the anger I was desperately trying to smother didn't have the power to kill anyone, particularly those I loved. Small wonder that I believed a dangerous girl was living inside me when I was eight years old who wanted me to take up a kitchen knife and kill my brother.

six

TOM OPENED UP a new world of nature to me during the months that followed. I rented the old farmhouse in Connecticut, excluding my old friends who were rightly upset about being disinvited, but I couldn't see how to weave them into my new life. It didn't take long for me to discover the pleasures of birding now that I was living with someone who got up at dawn to track spring warblers. Growing up in Brooklyn, I could at best recognize a robin and a sparrow and was thrilled to identify my first red-winged blackbird flying over a cornfield. Our only disagreement was on the subject of marriage — I was all for it, Tom was in no rush. I must have sulked a lot since we did marry that winter in a suite at the Plaza Hotel, with both families meeting for the first time. Having both of Tom's parents there meant a great deal to me since his mother, Helen, had been close to Ellen and had refused to meet me at first. His father, Dave, was more open and took me out to lunch to get to know me a bit. With his lifetime of practice as a labor mediator, he had skillfully negotiated a meeting between Helen and me that took place at their home in Paterson, New Jersey.

Instead of high drama, there was nothing but kindness. Dave sat me down in their sunroom and proudly pulled out a big dark red leather scrapbook filled with newspaper clippings of Tom's triumphs on the East Side High School basketball team. One headline, "Chuck Cole, Veteran of the Basketball Wars," caught my attention, as "Chuck" was the last name I expected Tom ever to have been dubbed. He had been named Charles Thomas Cole at birth, after Helen's dashing oldest brother who had sucked up all his siblings' earnings to finance his medical degree, then barely spoke with them ever again. When Charles Thomas was discovered to be a bigamist as well as the reputed lover of the flaming radical, Elizabeth Gurley Flynn, his family dropped the Charles part and forever after called his namesake just plain "Tommy."

The wish to make a feature film together never died, and within days of our marriage we set out to adapt *Joseph's Move*, a satirical novel Tom had recently completed. Inspired by Gogol's short story, "The Nose," it had as its hero a solitary man who becomes fixated on the idea that his life has been stolen from him by a golden-haired young insurance executive, Rollie Ralston, and who chases Rollie all over town trying to convince the executive to give his life back to him. Set in Boston, our hometown, we hoped to make it on a shoe-string using local actors. It looked more than possible that our wish would come true when a New York attorney found a group of private investors to finance the film, and Robert Redford, a tennis friend of Tom's, was intrigued enough with the script to consider playing the Rollie part. The day we were set to fly down to New York to sign the agreements, our attorney phoned just seconds before we were out the door. "Don't bother to come down, kids, the group has just decided to put their money in a sperm bank instead." It was laughable but a major blow, and any hopes of attaching Bob Redford quickly faded as well. He had just burst into stardom with *Butch Cassidy and the Sundance Kid* and moved far beyond our reach.

Unbeknownst to us, Martin Rosen, the producer of *Women in Love* and Tom's former literary agent, somehow found a copy of the screenplay and was eager to meet. When we got together at a New York restaurant full of hope that he would offer to finance our project, we were startled to learn that he had taken the liberty of showing the script to Richard Zanuck and David Brown, the co-heads of production at 20th Century Fox, without our knowledge and that the studio was ready to develop it with Martin as the producer. Tom, as writer, would receive $35,000 option money (the equivalent of $230,000 today) and considerably more if the film ever went into production. There was one hitch. I would have to withdraw as the director as the studio wanted one with lots of experience and an ability to attract top actors. As a consolation prize, Martin offered me the worthless role of associate producer. What I had at first considered another stroke of good luck was turning into my personal nightmare.

Poor Tom, he didn't know what to do. But I did — murder the man. What had started out as a small, independently financed movie written for me with love was about to be snatched away. Tom never pressured me, but knowing what a great opportunity this was for him, I let it all go, even though I had planned every shot in my head. I just couldn't stand in his way. I did my best to keep a smile on my face as Tom and I met with a series of some of Hollywood's best directors, each one excited by the script and each wanting to make the script less fantastical, the very quality that had attracted them to it in the first place.

Fortunately for me, all my desires suddenly swung in an entirely unpredictable direction; after spending just a long weekend with my three-year-old niece Jenny, I fell madly in love with her. By the time Tom and I arrived back home, I had become so overwhelmed with a longing for a child of my own, a feeling so entirely foreign to me, that I could think of little else. I had never had the slightest wish to become a mother and, except for watching over my little brother, had never done any babysitting. I was now thirty-three, considered old for having a first child. Tom was thirty-six. He had done his best to bury his own hopes for a child after Ellen was no longer able to bear one, but now they were set free to soar. At our next stay at the Connecticut farm, I tossed out my birth control pills. We were lucky on the first try.

I received the positive results at a small chemist's shop in London. Martin was living there and arranged for us to come over to work on a rewrite of *Joseph's Move*, both of us doing our best to become friends. As I stood there, absorbing the news, the unbidden thought, "I'll never be alone again," suffused me with a feeling of tranquility that was new to me. To this day, I'm not sure what I meant by the thought; Tom and I couldn't have been closer, I had friends, my parents loved me. All I knew was that the child and I would be bound to each other in a different way, a way I could not foresee. As I walked out of that little shop, I was almost floating.

Tom was overjoyed with the news, and the first weeks of my pregnancy went smoothly enough in spite of bouts of morning sickness until I started to bleed. A doctor advised complete bed rest, and after a few weeks of following his orders my pregnancy seemed stable enough for me to fly back to the States on my own. Midway through the flight, I began to bleed again, this time profusely, and found refuge in the bathroom, sure that my dream of becoming a mother was about to be flushed down a TWA chemical toilet. Fortunately, there was doctor on the plane; he had me lie down and saw me home with the same instructions given by the London doctor, "Do not move!" I could barely believe that the baby might still be alive in there, but it proved tenacious and held on. Tom came back immediately, and all was proceeding without further scares when Martin phoned with the shocking news that Zanuck and Brown had just been fired from Fox by its president, Zanuck's own father Daryl, and *Joseph's Move* was thereby cancelled.

Tom took it particularly hard, but I felt it less, since I had already been more or less pushed aside and was now immersed in reading baby books and fixing up a nursery. My mother was thrilled, hardly believing that I was actually having a child at that advanced age of thirty-four, and she came up to Cambridge to shop with me for baby clothes and blankets. Once we were getting close to my due date, Tom dutifully went with me to Lamaze classes to be my cheerleader as I practiced breathing away the expected pain of childbirth without painkillers, both of us part of that new 1970s frontier of couples ready to protect our newborns even if it killed us. A cheery instructor asked that we begin our lesson by introducing ourselves and testify why we had chosen to join the group. From the first couple on, it was the men who spoke, their large-bellied partners mute besides them. "Donna and I," then "Mary Beth and I," around half the circle. My ire was way up by the time it was our turn, especially as I had just been reading about a woman who had dared to climb the stage at a D.C. rally against the Vietnam War in an attempt to make her voice heard. Before she could get more than a few words out, a guy in the back of the audience yelled out, "Take her off the stage and fuck her," followed by ribald jokes and catcalls as though the men were at a burlesque show. Didn't she know that her proper place was in the back running off mimeographed copies of the men's speeches? Fortunately, the woman ahead of me in our circle did speak for herself, and I was spared from embarrassing myself by scolding the silent ladies for not speaking up when they were the stars of the show and not their husbands.

With the first exhilarating kick at five months, I'd had to admit to a lurking fear that had been growing inside me along with the baby. I worried that I would be irretrievably swept away into motherhood, as had happened to many women I knew, and that "Joyce the filmmaker" would cease to exist the second the baby was born. I got the idea, perhaps a bit crazy, that the only way I could prevent that erasure was to be contractually obligated to produce a film right after giving birth; I would then be "Joyce the filmmaker who happens to be a mother." When the offer to direct a documentary about an experimental school in Brooklyn suddenly came my way in my eighth month, I grabbed hold as if it were a life preserver.

I was telling my friend Barbara Norfleet, a sociologist teaching at Harvard, about the job I had just signed a contract for when she interrupted me with, "Forget *that* . . . Why don't you do a film about whether a woman's relationship with her mother changes when she has a baby of her own? You're in a unique position to document this. Use yourself and Tillie as the test subjects." To which I immediately replied, "You have got to be kidding. That would be the most narcissistic . . . " I don't think I even finished the sentence. Until then, documentary films took as their subject notable public events or famous people, and the thought of producing a film about a woman having a baby seemed outlandish.

Yet the more I thought about it, the more intrigued I became. I wish I could say that I was solely motivated by the feminist movement that was swirling around me. *Ms. Magazine* had just published its first issue, with Wonder Woman on its cover, and *Our Bodies,*

Ourselves was on every woman's nightstand. But though the feminist movement was certainly an influence, what excited me most was the chance to explore a new way of autobiographical storytelling, using the medium of film rather than the pen, something I didn't think had been done before. I knew that I wasn't interested in making the film Barbara suggested, but I did see the possibility of a film about the conflicts that would arise in my marriage, especially if I was going to continue my life as a working woman while being a new mother.

With little time left before my due date, I turned for funding to WNET in New York, and they thought the concept novel enough to promise me $10,000, half up front, half upon delivery (no pun intended). Now all I had left to do was produce the baby and find someone to do the filming for free. My hope was to break another barrier by collaborating with a female cinematographer, knowing full well that such a person might not exist; it was pretty much an all-male field. Luckily, Claudia Weill had recently graduated from Radcliffe College, had been using her boyfriend Eli Noyes's sync sound camera while making a few shorts with him, and was excited by the opportunity. My imagination was whirring with potential scenes, and as I talked all this over with my mother she reminded me about 8mm film footage taken at my Sweet Sixteen birthday party. It was disturbing for me to look at — the girl being celebrated looked so radiantly happy and threw into question why I remembered those early years as being ones of unremitting gloom. As I sat watching my old friends being twirled and dipped by their dancing partners, I also felt terribly stupid, that in my haste to flee Brooklyn I had let them drift completely out of my life. I knew that every one of them had married early and had babies I'd never met and now probably never would. It was an unsettling feeling. But that footage would give audiences an indelible sense of the life I had left behind.

I entered my tenth month with no sign of a child coming. A week passed, then one more and then another with my doctor assuring me that everything was perfectly normal. Since I had a hard time sleeping — my belly was far too big to lie on — Tom kept me company watching reruns of the *Sherlock Holmes Mystery Theater* well past midnight. Claudia and I had kept in touch daily and, just our luck, she was out of town as I went into labor around 2AM. Tom managed to stay calm enough to hustle me to the hospital and reach a standby crew who showed up just in time to film our baby's overdue entrance into our world. In spite of the Lamaze breathing techniques, it hurt like hell and helped me to forget that a camera was pointing straight between my legs. It helped even more that Tom had been allowed into the delivery room — another barrier breaker — and stood by my side, squeezing my hand in encouragement. Then, two amazing things happened at once: the baby slid out and the pain stopped instantly. I faintly heard the doctor announce "It's a girl," with Tom's voice jubilantly adding, "It's Sarah Rose!" When the nurse placed baby girl Sarah Rose in my arms seconds later, I was almost afraid to touch her, she was so new.

Like all first-time parents, we were overjoyed and sleepless and hopeless at following the rules laid out in every new parent's guidebook, Dr. Benjamin Spock's *Baby and Child Care*. The book, published in 1946 right after World War II, was in many ways a fantasy of how American life ought to be — every family with its own home, a front porch and a stay-at-home mom ready to wheel baby out to thrive in the unpolluted air. Yet somehow our daughter flourished in spite of our self-taught parenting, and I continued to work, producing both the *Block School* film and *Joyce at 34*, editing at home when Tom was there to be with the baby.

Claudia was filming the day I tried to cut a scene on my flatbed Steenbeck, a newly developed editing machine that allowed for comfortable sitting with a much larger viewing screen as well as multiple sound tracks. It was my turn to care for Sarah, so I had placed her on the floor beside me in a baby seat but she grew fussy the minute she saw me focusing exclusively on my work. My choice was either to quit for the day or pick her up and put her on my lap, hoping she would settle down. For a while it worked, the roll of film unspooling from one side of the editing table to another mesmerizing her. But I must have been dreaming to imagine my work problem would be solved so easily. Before I could stop her, Sarah's little hand suddenly shot out, grabbed for the nearest roll of film and put it in her mouth for just a little lick of the acetate, nearly cutting off a finger on her other hand as she excitedly slapped it up and down inches from the blade on the film splicer. It was one of the rare times I ever shouted, "Damn it!" to Sarah, whose only crime was curiosity, and I never tried that solution again. Instead, Tom and I did our civil best to agree on which of us most needed those extra hours to concentrate on our work.

The worst moments came when I got upset about housework, especially since I believed that my doing all the shopping and cooking was unfair. It was a joke, but bothersome just the same, that when he washed the dishes, I thanked him; when I washed the dishes, Tom would just walk away. I probably would have won my point sooner if I had followed the lead of the women in Aristophanes comedy, *Lysistrata*, who stopped having sex with their husbands until they, in turn, stopped going off to make war. After I don't know how many arguments, he finally saw the light of day. "It'll just be easier for me to go shopping and spend that hour and a half in the morning than to spend all my life fighting her." I doubted that either his father or mine had ever considered stooping to any such unmanly task. Taking out the garbage was their one generous exception to the rule.

The scene that turned out to exceed all my expectations and maybe the best part of the film was my mother's monthly luncheon with the retired and still feisty Brooklyn teachers she had worked with at PS 253 in Brighton Beach. It's certainly the most delightful. After the women had greeted each other, traded the latest photos of their grandkids and gossiped, I asked if I might pose a single question: "Did you ever feel conflicted about working and raising a family?" It was as though I had set off a bomb underneath their seats. Their answers came out in a rush. As hard as it is to believe now, it seems that in all the years they had eaten lunch together in the teacher's lunchroom, the women had never talked about it. Claudia and I knew, even as we were filming, that we were witnessing their consciousness "rising." All ten of them kept on talking excitedly, well after we had turned off the camera, interrupting each other with their own stories. "If I stay home, I'm bored, and that's not good for him. If I go to work, I come home tired, and that's not good for him either. Whatever we do is wrong." "If you found out you were pregnant, you had to leave at once!" My mother was finally able to get in a word or two edgewise: "One day, when I stayed home from school because I wasn't well, I heard the door open downstairs and my daughter, Joyce, calling out, 'Mommy, are you there? Oh, I'm so glad you're home, even though you're sick.'"

Joyce at 34 turned out to be a half-hour long, ending with Sarah Rose taking her first baby steps in the Boston Commons. In keeping with her arrival schedule, she didn't attempt this until she was fourteen months old, but, in her defense, she was already speaking more than a few words, and that compensated for her tardiness. When the film was broadcast on PBS in 1973, it was the first live birth ever seen on television, with my favorite comment coming when we were on Cape Cod for a few weeks' vacation. Someone told us about a nude beach, and Tom and I, with Sarah beside us, timidly removed our bathing suits and lay down on a blanket up near the sand dunes. When I sat up for a minute, I saw Claudia's parents, very proper Swiss, strolling naked, hand-in-hand, along the water's edge. Our eyes met, and they ambled towards us, smiling, as Tom and I quickly threw towels over our bodies. "But why are you covering yourself? You showed everything on public television!" said Claudia's father, making us all laugh with relief. Curiously, when I had "shown everything" on TV, I hadn't felt any embarrassment at all. The woman giving birth was just another character in a story. Being naked with a friend's parents was all too mortifyingly real.

The reviews were largely appreciative, the best from the *New York Times*. "This is not a feminist film, though clearly aware of feminist positions, but is a film about people of three generations and many loyalties and ambitions, and many ways of accommodating to life as a complex and viable continuum – and that insight is perhaps as close to ecstatic perception as the documentary film can get." I was excoriated by Ruby Rich, the Marxist film critic for the

Village Voice, for being privileged and not at all representative of most women. A perversely cherished reaction was from a man who walked out in disgust from a movie theater where the film was playing with a documentary about the investigative journalist I. F. Stone, muttering to his wife, "I want my money back. I thought it was a film about James Joyce, not some ugly dame having a baby!"

A curator from the Museum of Modern Art in New York must have seen the film because I got a letter from the museum's film library requesting a copy for their permanent collection, a most awesome request. Years later, Sarah Rose incorporated that event into a college essay that made me laugh out loud when she let me read it. "I was born on film. I have been born a dozen times on public television, once at a cross-cultural film festival in the Soviet Union, every year (so far as I know) at some or other university in the U.S. A roll of old celluloid, from which I could be born at any moment, is reposing in the vault at the *Museum of Modern Art.*" I now can't resist telling Sarah that she is "about to be born again" whenever I receive advance notice of a public screening, and she still smiles at my worn-out joke.

In 1973, the chances of *Joyce at 34* finding a distributor were less than zero. There were a number of companies that marketed films to public libraries and colleges but not one of them thought there was a large enough audience for documentaries about women's experiences to be profitable. Fortunately for me, a few other female directors, among them the now Academy Award–winning Julia Reichert, were having the same trouble with women-centered films, and they happened to meet up at the Flaherty Film Seminar in upstate New York. If no distributor wanted their movies, they boldly declared, they would distribute them on their own. Within weeks, New Day Films was born. When Claudia and I heard about this new cooperative we were eager to join. Jobs were split up, including the compiling of mailing lists, but it was up to each member to design, print and mail their own advertising brochures, for which we were lucky enough to get blurbs from Gloria Steinem and Shirley MacLaine. As we all suspected, there was a huge audience just waiting to be tapped, and the films caught on like wildfire in spite of there being just a few North American film festivals at which to showcase them, with most festivals not starting up until almost twenty years later in the 1990s. Each 16mm print that I put in a film can and hand-carried to the post office felt like a small victory.

Back in Brooklyn on a visit home, I expressed my excitement about the advancement woman would soon make in every field to my father, who replied, "It will never happen. Men will never give up their power." I tried laughing, but how right he was in so many ways, ways I was to come up against later on. *Joyce at 34* had just won a blue ribbon at the prestigious American Film Festival, and an article in *Variety* reported that, for the first time in the Festival's history, women had won more than half of the documentary film awards. A cause for celebration! Then the writer went on to deliver a heavy dose of reality: women had won the documentary awards because very little money had been involved in making them; it was highly unlikely that film studios would ever trust women with the larger sums needed to produce a feature. We were emotionally unstable.

I did my best to ignore both the *Variety* article and my father's pessimistic warnings, but, in truth, my chances for raising funding for documentaries was far more realistic than for features. Within months, I was putting my energies into finding a way to continue my experiment with the kind of personal storytelling I had employed with *Joyce at 34*, sketching out in my mind an ambitious series of films about girls and women at different life stages. I had heard about EDC, a company in nearby Watertown that was a forerunner in developing math and science curriculum for schools, and though getting them interested in moviemaking was a long shot, I made an appointment to meet Adeline Naiman, the person in charge of their innovative programming. I was instantly taken with Adeline, especially as she was wearing a bright red Marimekko dress and spoke faster than I did. Her mind worked just as fast, and within minutes she grasped the novelty of my idea, grew excited at the prospect of producing films (which would be a new adventure for her) and was quite sure she could secure funding from the National Institute of

Education. True to Adeline's promise, enough money came through by the end of the year to begin our first film.

I had always been troubled by the way girls behaved around boys when they entered their teen years and found a nearby junior high school in Waltham that was willing to let us film there for a few months. It seemed as though time had stopped; it was 1974, but I might as well have been in my 1940s classroom since so little had changed. With camerawoman Joan Weidman, whom I'd met through Claudia, I followed a trio of twelve-year-old girls, all of them excited and nervous about the prospect of becoming freshmen in a co-ed school. We filmed them getting better and better at flirting with boys and, as I'd feared, dumbing down right before our eyes, with Diane, the best scholar among them, asking to transfer into an easier math class because she suddenly found the work too hard. Mary Anne, the girl with the wicked smile, eagerly went out for cheerleading while the boys her age joined the football team, where their coaches screamed at them to be more manly and aggressive. With fathers who expected them to get married and stay home to raise babies as their mothers and older sisters were doing, it would be hard for any of these girls to imagine alternative futures for themselves. Small wonder that Mary Anne claimed that she hated to be serious because it gave her a headache. When finished, we titled the film *Girls at 12* and, after it aired on PBS stations, we entered it into the prestigious American Film Festival and were excited when it won a top prize.

From the beginning, Adeline and I believed it was important that our series be multiracial, and our next film, *Clorae and Albie,* featured two Black women, best friends since childhood, who were both smart and irreverently funny. At the age of twenty-one, their closeness was in danger of collapsing as Albie attended college while Clorae took care of her three children on her own. But Clorae wasn't the kind of person who could be held back for long; staying at home with little company but toddlers was driving her crazy. She not only took a part time job at McDonald's but also started attending a prep academy to get her GED, all with the help of a parent-run day care center close by. My being white didn't seem to keep them from acting freely around me or talking about race. To help make vivid one of her more painful experiences, Albie asked that we film her trudging up a hill at the all-white college in Vermont where she been given a full scholarship. As the only Black person enrolled, she was so lonely she quit after her first year. When it was time to interview Albie, instead of asking her to sit and respond to my questions about her life while looking into the camera, I was inspired to try a less traditional way. She talked about the history of each pair of shoes lined up in her bedroom closet, when she had purchased them, where she had worn them, with many memories rushing back just by holding them in her hands. When she was done, I knew it was the most satisfying interview I had ever filmed. I learned far more about Albie than I had imagined possible, and all without having to ask a a single question.

Like *Girls at 12*, *Clorae and Albie* wasn't as easy to edit as *Joyce at 34*, which had its own sort of beginning, middle and end: a baby is born, sits up and finally walks. But once I settled on a beginning, a structure fell into place, with each scene revealing more and more about these young women's lives. Instead of a clear dramatic arc, the momentum came from an engagement with characters you cared about. I could only hope that the foundation grants would keep coming and that Adeline and I would be filming women into their ninth decade and beyond.

seven

I WAS WORKING LATE in the editing room, preparing for a sound mix for our next film, featuring Sally Garcia, a married forty-year-old mother whose four kids found it hilarious that she thought herself capable of getting a paying job, when I was interrupted by the ringing telephone. "How would you like to go to Nigeria in two weeks?" Nancy Boggs, a program director at the Ford Foundation whom I'd met while seeking extra funding, was on the line, and her question, like Ricky Leacock's about going to South Dakota, was so far-fetched that I thought I had misheard her. She quickly explained that the foundation had been supporting the work of a visionary pediatrician, Olikoye Ransome-Kuti, who was setting up rural health clinics in Nigeria to serve as models for how to save the lives of the country's children, half of whom were dying before they were five from easily preventable diseases. Since it was the rare physician who was willing to give up a lucrative practice in the big cities, the clinics were being staffed by local villagers trained to recognize common disease symptoms and offer simple remedies. Nancy knew that it was highly doubtful that a written report on Ransome-Kuti's work would have an impact on the government's health ministry and persuaded the foundation to release funding for a film that might break through their wall of neglect.

I hesitated for barely an instant. How could I say no to this opportunity to be of help, especially as it had always been my dream to adventure far away. Assuming that I might be reluctant to travel on my own, she asked if Tom would be willing to accompany me and help with a shooting plan. He was as eager as I was when I relayed the request. Completely ignorant, without even a notion of where Nigeria was on a map, the first thing I did when I arrived home was to pull out a world atlas and identify all the places Nancy had mentioned. Two separate trips were planned, the first to visit the clinics and make the necessary arrangements, the second for me to go, without Tom, and film with an all-female crew since most women in the Muslim north were in *purdah*. Husbands were the only males allowed inside the compounds where their multiple wives were kept in seclusion.

Sarah and her best friend, Peter, were fascinated by the disease names they heard Tom and me trying to pronounce and, one afternoon, I heard them shouting *Schistosomiasis!*, *Trypanosomiasi!*, in the back of the house. They were playing at being fierce warriors, stomping out their enemies underfoot. As I watched their flushed faces, I thought, "I'm mad to think I can be away from my daughter for three weeks, she's barely five years old," even though we had hired a lovely and responsible student to care her for. I had heard frightening stories about the military police in Nigeria, but not too deep down I knew the real truth. I suffered from an unreasoning fear of someone kidnapping my beloved daughter, or even worse, that she might vanish into thin air. It had started right after she had learned to walk.

I had gone to the beach with a friend, in fact the mother of Sarah's pal, Peter, and asked that she keep an eye on Sarah while I went off to fetch something from my car. When I returned moments later, I saw Doreen busily chatting with another woman with Peter digging in the sand beside her. Sarah was nowhere in sight. In an instant, the sound went out of the universe. All I could see were the ocean waves beating against the shore. I started running along the water's edge, frantic, my eyeballs whirling in every direction. In what seemed like an eternity but was probably no more than a few minutes, I saw her toddling up ahead, having a fine time exploring the world on her own. That terror never left me, and I have had to fight against keeping Sarah close by even as she grew older. I almost didn't make it out of Boston the night of our departure. The minute I started walking to the check-in counter at Logan I had a massive panic attack and would have fled back home if Tom hadn't cajoled me onto the plane.

Our first encounter with life in Nigeria actually occurred in Rome where we had a stopover for the night. Our flight to Lagos was scheduled to leave at four the next afternoon, giving us time for a leisurely lunch in the nearby Piazza Navona. This would be my first time in Rome, and I intended to enjoy every second of it. We had barely ordered when we saw the worried face of the hotel's concierge scanning the crowd. Hurrying to our table, he told us that Nigeria Airways had phoned the hotel with news that the plane was leaving two hours ahead of schedule. After a mad scramble to grab our luggage and a mad taxi ride to the airport, we were astonished that the Nigerian passengers waiting in the departure lounge seemed in no hurry at all. They knew from experience that, far from an early departure, we would be lucky if the plane left at all.

Five hours later, all 150 of us finally boarded buses to shuttle us out to the waiting plane. The second the bus doors swung open, Tom and I were almost knocked to the ground as the Nigerians ran towards the airplane steps. It was only later that we learned that the airline had no reliable way of knowing how many seats they sold for any flight. Nigeria's capital, Lagos, had been built on land dredged up from the sea, and all attempts at placing computer and telephone cables underground had so far proved futile, rotting away before the job was even completed. Overbooking was common, and if you were unlucky enough to occupy the last seat when a minister sauntered on board, you could be bounced off. But in the end we made it on, and everyone settled in rather peacefully.

The plane landed at dusk, and as soon as we cleared customs we were swarmed by ragged men and boys wanting to help with our bags. The Ford Foundation driver was nowhere in sight. We waited, rather calmly at first, then began to get nervous as the crowd thinned and the light began to fade. A few drivers with beat-up taxis beckoned to us, but a sweeper warned that if we rode with one of them, "They will slit your throat, take your money and dump you by the side of the road." Hours later and well past midnight, we were the only passengers left waiting at the curb with our two suitcases; the entire airport had closed down, the place deserted as a graveyard. Given what the sweeper had told us, I was increasingly sure we wouldn't make it through the night. Suddenly, what seemed an illusion, a green bus with a Nigeria Airways, logo glowing brightly above the windshield, came rattling toward us. Its door opened with a *whoosh,* and my eyes immediately went straight to the razor blade hanging from the smiling driver's neck on a thin gold chain. Just as I was about to turn and run for my life, an angel from heaven appeared in the form of a sleepy young woman who sat up, yawning, probably his girlfriend. With an immense sigh of relief, we stepped on board.

The journey into Lagos was a vision out of Dante's *Inferno,* with open sewers on both sides of the road flanked by mounds of burning garbage six feet high, the bright flames illuminating the baskets of live chickens, yams and cassava being carried on the heads of the men and women walking into the capital. I was so mesmerized by the scene outside, I almost fell off my seat when the driver suddenly pulled to a stop at "the number one best hotel in the city," its exterior as shabby as its lobby would prove to be. The one desk clerk still on duty informed us, in his most sorrowful tones, that all the rooms were taken except for the Bridal Suite. It was an obvious falsehood, but we hadn't yet learned the Nigerian art of bargaining, so we immediately said that we'd take it. The second Tom and I were inside, we bolted the door and drank half the bottle of Macallan Scotch whiskey we had brought as a present for Ransome-Kuti, the doctor who had set up the clinics, and passed out.

The next morning, we set out on foot to find the Ford Foundation office, amazing the small staff that greeted us. It seems that a secretary thought we were arriving on a morning flight and had indeed sent a driver to pick us up, but when he reported that we were not on the flight, she promptly forgot about us. Now the mix-up no longer seemed important, our minds focused on finding Ransome-Kuti as quickly as possible. Our first meeting took place inside the children's ward at the Lagos University Teaching Hospital, a sight that is hard to prepare oneself for — crib after crib of malnourished babies, their ribs protruding, crying their little hearts out while their distraught parents who had trekked in from miles away hovered over them, hoping to catch a physician's eye. I felt undone by it all and couldn't but marvel at the nurses and doctors doing their best to help these very sick children while maintaining their own composure.

It was easy to spot our doctor, a commanding-looking man who came from a remarkable family. His mother, Funmilayo Kuti, a woman rights campaigner, was the first Nigerian woman to drive a car and a member of the team that negotiated Nigerian independence from the British. His father, an Anglican priest, was said to have flogged a white colonial inspector who insulted him at a time when Nigerians were expected to treat their British overlords like demigods. His first cousin was the Nobel Prize–winning author, Wole Soyinka. Most famous of all was his younger brother, Fela, a musician and a founder of Afrobeat.

The night before we were to start on our journey to visit the rural clinics, Koye (as Ransome-Kuti was known to his friends) took us to see his notorious brother and his all-female backup singers, the Queens, perform on an outdoor stage at the family compound. Only months before, Fela had released the album *Zombie*, a scathing attack on Nigerian soldiers, using the zombie metaphor to describe the country's military. A smash hit, the album had infuriated the government, setting off a vicious attack, with one thousand soldiers attacking the commune Fela had established in the family's home. Fela was severely beaten and the now elderly Funmilayo Kuti was thrown out of a second story window by a crazed soldier, dying from her wounds within days. Undaunted, Fela not only continued to perform but married all twenty-seven Queens in a traditional Yoruba ceremony as a way of offering them financial protection. We were seated right below the stage, and it was eerie to be looking up at the window out of which Fela and Koye's mother had been thrown to her death.

Hundreds of exhilarated men danced to the music under glowing colored bulbs looped between the trees. The Afrobeat was so irresistible that Tom got up, eager to join in the dancing, holding out his hand to me, but I couldn't join in, overwhelmed by the force of so much male energy surrounding me. Except for the Queens, there wasn't a single other female in sight.

A chauffeured Ford Foundation car was waiting to pick us up at dawn, and I couldn't have been happier to leave Lagos behind and set out to visit the clinics. The roads we travelled on were dangerous, not only because of the potholes big as craters but also because drivers rushed through the intersections at high speed, daring each other to chicken out. The military checkpoints along the way were even scarier, but Dr. Owolabe, our guide and translator, taught us a simple lesson to help get past the armed soldiers who thumbed our passports with suspicious eyes: "Tell them your life story, starting with where you were born, all about your brothers and sisters until you become real people to them." It invariably worked.

The village health workers Tom and I met during our journey were inspiring in their devotion to their work and helped us to gauge what would be most important to film when I returned. I soon realized that without telephones my arrival plans would often have to be rather unusual: "Let's meet by this tree four weeks from today in the afternoon," hoping that when I returned they would actually be there, and happily they almost always were. The two weeks flew by, and, the second we were out of the taxi back home, Sarah jumped into my arms and wouldn't let go, eager to tell us about all her adventures while we had been away. We both were so at ease with my leaving the second time, especially as Tom would be with her, that she simply gave me a hurried kiss goodbye the morning of my next departure, saying, "Have a good time in Nigeria, Mommy," and rushed off to join her kindergarten classmates.

I would be gone for four weeks this time, but, instead of being filled with anxiety, I was looking forward to the adventure, especially as Joan Weidman, my wonderful cameraperson, would be travelling with me along with Nancy Schreiber, a rare female gaffer to handle the lighting and Debra Franco to record the sound. Flying out of Kennedy, we checked fifty cases of camera, sound, and lighting equipment, much of it doubled in case of breakage, all of which had to be loaded into its own separate van that trailed behind us as we travelled around the Nigerian countryside, with my crew getting inventive when telling their own family histories to the soldiers who often stopped us along the way.

My companions had experienced the same shock of displacement that I had when first arriving, but they recovered their good humor as a sort of reverence took hold among us for the nurse practitioners we met, women who were doing their best to educate the hundreds of thousands of villagers who knew almost nothing about the sources of the diseases that were plaguing them. Most remarkable of all was the near saintly Sister Comfort Imoke, who had started a small hospital in southern Nigeria's Cross River State with her physician husband but soon realized that it was too difficult for ill people to reach them. Now she was going out to where the people lived, bringing along the flock of local girls that she had trained as nurse's assistants. With folding exam tables, benches and a host of medical paraphernalia, the girls marched into the villages with Sister Comfort in the lead, often joined by dozens of local women, all singing to celebrate the arrival of the roving outdoor clinic. The babies cradled in their arms were as sick as the ones that brought me to tears in the Lagos Teaching Hospital, but, now that I was filming, I had to put a freeze on my empathy. My entire focus had to be on capturing all the elements of the scene before my eyes.

I was constantly amazed at the inventiveness displayed by the villagers themselves. At one thatched-roof clinic, the teaching was done through staging little plays, with the aides playing sick people seeking help, much to the delight of the local villagers. In Kano, an ancient city in the Muslim north, most men, even those of modest means, had four wives living together in mud-walled compounds, the husband being the only male allowed inside. At a "Men's Club," when a nurse asked a representative of the emir who was sitting up front to order the men to let their wives visit the new health clinic without their permission, there was a lot of embarrassed laughter all around as they were all guilty as charged. Unfortunately, I saw the danger of that restriction firsthand when we filmed one of the visiting nurses doing her best to bring down the fever of a dehydrated infant whose distraught fourteen-year-old mother hadn't dared leave her compound for fear her husband would divorce her, leaving her and her baby destitute. The distress of the baby and mother was so terrible to watch, we had to turn off our camera.

The hardest part of my job was keeping my crew's spirits up, since my own often flagged under the strain. I knew the women were all being well paid, but I doubt they had imagined how rough it would be. We were continually hungry, and the places we slept in were crawling with bugs, often an inch long. If only I had thought to bring along a cassette player, I could have played rock music in the evenings for us to dance to. Instead, we took to doodling cartoons with the Sharpies we brought along to label our film cans, competing to see which of us could be the most outrageous. Joan easily took first prize with one she titled *Queen Enthroned on a Toilet.* Below the title was a crowned Royal Highness seated on a commode gleefully crushing a giant insect underneath her royal foot with the motto, *Even as I Shit I Kill,* writ large on her family crest.

I should have kept the live chicken that one tribal chief offered me as a going away present since I could have had it roasted at the Chinese restaurant with impossible-to-find fresh vegetables that we stumbled upon the next day. I still blush to admit the positively ridiculous thing I said to the chief when we first met. Arriving late at night, he had welcomed us with great solemnity and invited me to sit opposite him and his council of elders in a semicircle. It was pitch black, with barely enough light from a glowing fire to see the men's faces. It became instantly clear that they thought I was a doctor travelling with my nurses and would cure their many illnesses. I started to explain that, no, I was there to make a movie about their clinic and wanted his permission before we began, but I started to trail off as I read the growing disappointment in their faces. I became so flustered that when one of the elders asked where I had come from, I actually heard myself answering, "I come from across the waters," and I raised my arm to gesture to a land far, far away. I could hear my crew laughing behind me. I was glad it was so dark since my face had turned bright red.

The clinic I had put last to visit because it was the most difficult to reach was in the far north, near Maiduguri, a city then unknown to most westerners and now famous for being the site of deadly Boko Haram kidnappings. Since it was so far away, I decided to charter two small planes, one for my crew and one for our fifty cases, knowing there was no way of guaranteeing four airplane seats on the same commercial flight, let alone safe passage for our equipment. I was leery of our pilot even before we took off — a German straight out of a World War II movie who played up his derring-do self for the benefit of us ladies. But his constant patter stopped being even remotely amusing when he flew the plane into a thunderstorm and was clearly entertained by our terror. Thankfully, the sun came out just as we landed and we scrambled out, the pilot bidding us a jaunty farewell.

Looking around, I realized he had deposited us on an empty strip thousands of feet from the deserted terminal. The other pilot had already landed and departed, leaving our metal equipment cases unattended and broiling in the blazing sun. I was stunned; he didn't seem to care that the exposed film inside the cases would be irretrievably ruined if left there much longer. With no one from the clinic to meet us, never mind a baggage handler or cart, we spent the next hour lugging the heavy cases into the shade. By now we were thirsty, and there was no choice but to walk into Maiduguri and try to find a few drivers with cars. Debbie volunteered to go with me, not offering much protection, since she was smaller than me, and neither of us could speak even a word in the local language.

There were only men on the streets, which were considered unsafe for unaccompanied women, and they paused whatever they were doing to stare silently at us as we passed by. I was scared stiff. Finally, through gesture and pointing, we made ourselves understood to one man who found two beat-up vans that just might make it on the final hundred-kilometer journey. The final hour over gutted fields was so rough that we had to unpack the camera lenses and pay the children who trailed after us to carry them on their heads. Once we arrived, the villagers were more than welcoming, the women inviting us to share their huts and meals. We did give them a shock when we began to eat in the presence of men, and far from being envious of our freedom to go where we pleased, they felt sorry that we had to carry so much equipment on our backs. As for our white skin, they admitted with some laughter that they found all four of us rather ugly.

What should have been the high point of our journey — finally going home — was the complete opposite. Arriving at Lagos International Airport after an exhausting four weeks, ready to sink into our airplane seats and sleep for hours, we learned that all flights had just been cancelled. A plane had crashed on the only runway and could not be cleared away until a Lloyd's of London insurance adjuster arrived to examine the scene. We settled in, expecting it would be a matter of hours. Our wait turned into three nightmarish days, by which time thousands of hysterical travelers were offering bribes to anyone who looked even remotely official. The vendors were out of food and water, and the toilets were soon overstuffed. Even a plastic chair to sit on was prized. There was little point in dragging ourselves back to Lagos since planes might resume flying at any minute, and we'd have no way of knowing. Finally, an officer from the Ford Foundation office came out to check on us just as rumor spread that a Swiss Air flight would be leaving shortly. With the man from Ford at my side, I rushed to the ticket counter minutes before it opened for business and began to tell my life story. That, along with some money slipped into an envelope, worked wonders. Within minutes, all four of us were on board. After the airport's chaos, the plane was a marvel of quiet and comfort. Then, at my stopover at Zurich Airport for the night, I experienced another marvel: the taxi driver stopped for a light with not a single other car in sight.

Koye was an easy houseguest when he came to work with us in Cambridge and record the narration for the film. Only six months had passed, but I had been missing his company and his gift for storytelling. He had but one complaint: it was so quiet that he had barely slept, Lagos being the noisiest city in the world. In this, he was my complete opposite. I gladly took my bedside radio and put it next to his pillow. The finished film, released in 1978 to multiple international health agencies, must have made a strong impression on the Nigerian government. They appointed our esteemed doctor minister of health a few years later. Fearless in every way, Koye broke the conspiracy of silence surrounding the raging AIDS epidemic in his country by announcing that his brother Fela had died from Kaposi's sarcoma brought on by AIDS. The nation was stunned. No one had dared speak the word "AIDS" aloud before, but Koye's announcement highlighted the military government's almost criminal failure to address the crisis. More than a half a million people attended the funeral near the site of the family compound.

eight

T HAT MONTH IN Nigeria had been my longest time away from Sarah, but happily both of us survived. Now when I went to meetings, I took her along since she would readily settle down in a corner with a book. Then, when she was about eight, we changed her life dramatically when Tom and I decided to leave Cambridge and move to a small town in northwestern Connecticut. We had been taking occasional trips there to visit a sculptor friend of Tom's, Philip Grausman, who was restoring an old house he had just purchased with his wife, the choreographer Martha Clarke. On our visits, Sarah and Tom were content to sit by Phil's side as he sculpted from clay while I watched Martha fooling around with new ideas for dance in a studio built above the ramshackle barn. She had just left Pilobolus Dance Theater, of which she was a founding member, to strike out on her own, a somewhat risky adventure. When we all got together for dinner, one of us floated the idea of doing a film about where ideas for art come from. The wine helped. When we got back to Cambridge, Tom and I wrote up a brief proposal that outlined a plan to film Martha over the next year, seeing where her dance experiments would lead her — the why of the choices she made in music, in costume and set design. It would be a very different film from the ones I had already made, which basically followed the ways people went about their lives. The challenge here would be to find a visual vocabulary to convey Martha's creative mind.

I knew of only one person that might be interested in this kind of unusual filmmaking: David Loxton at WNET's Independent Documentary Fund. When I went to meet him at his office in one of those old warehouse buildings on lower Broadway, I found a most energetic and amiable man, and, as he was a huge Pilobolus fan, my job of selling our idea to him was easier than any film I have ever pitched. It was no wonder, as he had also nurtured memorable video art with Nam June Paik and many other early innovators of the form. I had assumed before I went to the meeting that I would have to write lengthy applications to various foundations for funding, which entailed days of tedious work, then wait for many months before finding out if I was successful. You can imagine my astonishment when I learned that same day that the Documentary Fund was supported by the National Endowment for the Arts and that David could allocate money to us immediately.

Collaborating with Martha that next year was always intriguing, and, though we worked in completely different mediums, at bottom our methods were the same: we both worked off images we came across — a photograph, a painting — and we both strung moments together to make a whole, often not knowing where we might land. Curiously, as I cut together these mini-scenes of her explorations, the film took on a structure not unlike my other documentaries: an idea is born, it develops and, in this case, it ends with Martha performing a complete dance with two male partners set to a Schubert piano trio and filmed in one continuous take with the cameraman, Don Lenzer, uncannily anticipating the dancers' every move. Though millions of people viewed the film on PBS, that number was abstract and couldn't possibly afford me the pleasure I took in seeing it on a much larger screen at the American Film Festival, surrounded by a live audience of two hundred and hearing their applause when it won a blue ribbon.

It had dawned on me while filming how happy I would be living in the countryside within striking distance of Manhattan, something that Tom had been pushing for. With Phil's help, we found a fifties house we didn't love in nearby Kent that made up for its oddities by being situated over a waterfall with a large rose garden outside the kitchen door. I remember thinking that a rose garden was for old ladies but was converted when their first blooms appeared and spent our first winter poring over catalogues. I even got into baking

Christmas cookies, with Sarah as the chief decorator, and making jam from our gooseberry bushes. And, of course, we planted a vegetable garden. Unfortunately, the deer jumped over our fence, and the rabbits burrowed underneath.

Tom's father had died a few years earlier, and Helen had stayed on in the family home in Paterson by herself. The house was situated on the edge of a small park where Helen had taken her children sledding in happier years past, but the house was now a target for burglars. We feared for her safety and wanted her to move — she had already been locked into her garage by teenagers who stole the remote and broke into the house — but she and Dave had lived there for more than fifty years, and she couldn't imagine living anywhere else. When we found that a condo in the center of Kent was available for sale, we rushed over to look at it. It was a duplex unit, one of four, with views of the surrounding countryside. Best of all, two of the neighboring units were owned by Wanda and Vladimir Horowitz, one for living in when they came for country weekends, and the other for the maestro to practice in. The unit that was available for purchase was right next to the one with his piano.

Helen loved the apartment, especially loved the idea of being close to Tom and a young granddaughter, could hardly believe she would be hearing Horowitz playing as though he were in her living room. Wanda was very gracious when she moved in, but the maestro was never seen. The not-too-improbable story going round was that Horowitz had been bitten by a mosquito getting out of a car on their first visit and fled back to Manhattan, never to return. The youngest daughter of Arturo Toscanini, Wanda's scowl was legendary, and she inherited her father's temper. "My father made me neurotic, and my husband made me crazy," she told us one afternoon over tea. I never found her easy but became rather fond of her as one might be of the Duchess in *Alice in Wonderland*. My mother-in-law was the complete opposite and very easy to love. The pleasure that she took in daily things made one want to be in her company. Still active, she frequently picked up Sarah at school and would keep her when we had to be away.

One night, Tom and I were driving home from New York when he pulled to a stop at the only traffic light in our small town. It was near midnight, not another car or pedestrian in sight. I was half asleep in the passenger seat when Tom suddenly rolled down his window and looked up at the sky, amazed. "Quick, you've got to look at this!" I leaned past him, and what I saw about a thousand feet up was straight out of a sci-fi movie: an elongated, oval-shaped UFO with white lights running along its outer edges. It hovered in place for about ten more seconds and then zoomed away over the hills. Tom instantly put his foot on the gas and took off to chase it. "No, no, I don't want to be kidnapped by aliens, please, you have to turn back." He stopped the car, and we just sat there for a while, totally bewildered, comparing descriptions of what each of us had seen. They were identical. When we were finally home and Sarah was safely in bed, we called a few police stations in the area to see if anyone had reported similar sightings. I suspect they put us down as crank callers.

Then another unexpected thing happened, but it was all too terrestrial; my period was late. At first, I didn't think too much about it, but after two more weeks went by and no trace of it appeared, I began to think the unthinkable. Was I pregnant at forty-four? It was remotely possible since I had stopped taking birth control pills a few years back when reports of their causing blood clots became public and had gone back to using the less foolproof diaphragm, in spite of loathing it. Fortunately, home pregnancy test kits had recently become available, thus sparing the lives of millions of female rabbits that had been injected with urine from potentially pregnant humans, then sliced open to see if their ovaries were enlarged. And instead of waiting days for the results, I could have the results within two hours of purchasing the kit at the local pharmacy.

Tom and I did our best to keep our nervousness in check but couldn't stop glancing at the small test tube that contained my urine now combined with a mysterious chemical agent. According to instructions, if I were pregnant, a brown donut-shaped ring would appear at the bottom of the tube. I didn't know what to pray for. Ten

years earlier, I was consumed by my desire to have a child; now . . .
I just didn't know what I felt. It would have been wonderful if we
had given Sarah a little baby sister or brother when she was younger,
but now that she was almost ten years old and I forty-four . . .

When the brown ring appeared looking exactly like the picture in
the instruction sheet, I was stunned. I don't know how long I stood
there frozen in our small bathroom, but I remember Tom taking the
test tube from my hand and, drawing me close to him, not saying a
word. It had seemed so unlikely that I was pregnant that we hadn't
really talked about what we might do if it were true. Instead, we had
joked about the probability of having a baby with two enormous
heads since we were well past our youth. But suddenly, all the nervous
jokes were no longer funny: every fiber in my body could remember
the bliss of holding a newborn in my arms. But I instantly knew it was
not to be. Not because Tom and I were too old. The life we had made
together had allowed us to explore the kind of writing and moviemaking that often paid very little, to travel to distant lands or, in Tom's
case, regional theaters when a play of his was in rehearsal. A new baby
would change all that dramatically. Even if we could afford a nanny, I
doubted I would want to leave a precious child for the first few years.
As I stood there, I also knew that a clock was ticking inside me; if I was
going to terminate the pregnancy, I needed to do it as soon as possible
before that cluster of cells grew any larger.

What a difference twenty some odd years make. The landmark
Supreme Court decision, *Roe v. Wade*, in 1973 had made abortion
legal. Instead of slinking around like a criminal, unsure if I would
live to tell the tale, we deposited Sarah at Grandma Helen's on a
sunny morning, telling them both we had a meeting to attend, and
drove an hour to the Hartford hospital where friendly staff took care
of all my needs. We were back home by late afternoon. As I lay in
bed to rest, I could hear Sarah rattling around the house, singing to
herself, and felt very sad. A window to another kind of life had been
opened very briefly for me, and I had closed it.

I was on my own one afternoon when, once again, a telephone
call would change the direction of my life. Unlike the other calls

from people that I had worked with before, this one was from a complete stranger. The man at the other end of the line introduced himself as Philip Handleman and asked for Tom, wanting to congratulate him on winning a nationwide competition with his play, *Medal of Honor Rag*. The prize offered was a filmed production for the new series, *American Playhouse*, on PBS. "Oh, how wonderful" I spluttered, "Are you calling from PBS?" "No, I'm not associated with them. I saw a production in Detroit, thought it so important that I submitted it on my own." Martin Rosen and *Joseph's Move* flashed through my head. "Did you secure the rights from Tom's agent, Lois Berman?" "No, I haven't." I was now speechless, especially when he assumed that Tom would be eager to go with him to a meeting with the series executive producers in Washington, D.C., at the end of the week.

Tom had written the play Mr. Handleman was talking about at the height of the Vietnam War, almost ten years earlier, when to his father's dismay he had taken the radical step of quitting his job in MIT's literature department just as he was about to be tenured; he had found it impossible to both write and teach at the same time. What gave Tom the final push towards the risky move was a story that he read in the *New York Times* that deeply troubled him. Dwight Johnson, the only Black soldier in our nation's history to receive the Congressional Medal of Honor at that time, had just been killed in a grocery store holdup in a white section of Detroit by a storeowner who claimed that Johnson had pointed a gun at him, though the police never found a weapon.

Driven to discover what had led a war hero, with no criminal record and cash in his pocket, to end up in a morgue with five bullet wounds in his body, Tom interviewed returning Vietnam veterans and, in doing so, learned about a then medically unrecognized illness, post-traumatic stress disorder. Dwight Johnson's own story was heartbreaking. Raised as a devout Christian, an altar boy and an Eagle Scout, he was drafted into the army at nineteen and sent off to fight in a war he barely understood. He had grown close to the other soldiers in his tank, and exactly one day before his tour of duty was up, was randomly assigned to another tank. The morning of his final day in Vietnam, the tank he should have been in with his buddies was blown to smithereens right before his eyes. Horrified, he hoisted himself out of his undamaged tank and tried to pull his trapped friends from the flaming metal. It was too late. All he could see was bits of their charred flesh, and he went berserk. Armed only with a .45-caliber pistol, he hunted the Vietnamese through the trees, killing twenty of them. It took three shots of morphine and a straitjacket to quiet him down. Within forty-eight hours, he was released and flown back to Detroit on a commercial US airline with no follow-up treatment planned.

Tom knew that, in attempting to turn Johnson's story into a play, he was tackling a big story about survivor guilt, about trying to reconcile the conflict between a deep Christian faith and being rewarded by your country for killing. The play opened at the Theater de Lys in New York in 1976 to strong reviews. Tillie and all the wonderful ladies I had filmed just five years before showed up for the first Wednesday matinee and were moved to tears. Although it ran only for thirteen weeks before closing, it continued to be performed in regional theaters for many years. Philip Handleman was one of the thousands of audience members who had seen it that way.

Tom was as taken aback as I had been when I told him about the unusual phone call. With a bit of research, we found out that the Handleman family was quite wealthy, having earned millions with a monopoly on record sales to chain stores. Tom was in a quandary. If he gave Philip the TV rights and didn't disclose to PBS that the man had submitted the play illegally, he could be heading for serious trouble; if he refused, he was afraid of losing out on an audience of millions. After deciding to play along for a while, he asked me to fly down with him to D.C. where he had arranged to meet Philip in advance of a meeting with PBS. It didn't take long to realize that things were not going to end well when Tom held out his hand in greeting and Philip declined, mumbling something about germs.

When the three of us arrived at PBS, I was pleasantly surprised to find that I knew Dave Davis, one of the executive producers, from his days at the head of the Ford Foundation when I made the Nigeria film and under whose auspices *American Playhouse* had just been created. He congratulated Tom on his play and introduced us all to Lindsay Law, the other producer who would actually be the one running the *Playhouse* series. The meeting went fairly smoothly until Lindsay, upon learning that Philip had neither film or television experience, asked if I would be the hands-on producer. Philip stiffened and replied that he would consider it. A few days later, the phone rang, once again, with Philip on the line. In very few words, he informed me that I wasn't "good enough" to be part of his production team, that he would manage very well on his own, "thank you very much," and hung up. This time I wasn't speechless; I was outraged. Tom's first reaction was to give the whole thing up, but once we both cooled down, I offered to spill the beans to Lindsay and see what he suggested we do.

When I confessed the whole story, Lindsay was amused and assured me that we could proceed as sole producers, suggesting we offer Philip the infamous associate producer credit. Of course, Philip was furious and threatened to sue us. He hired an attorney at one of the top law firms in Manhattan, hoping to intimidate us, but we went ahead anyway. Lloyd Richards, the man who brought Lorraine Hansberry's *Raisin in the Sun* to Broadway and would later do the same with August Wilson's ten play *Pittsburgh Cycle*, agreed to direct. Lloyd was a formidable presence, and being somewhat in awe of him at our first meeting, I waited patiently for him to answer a question I had put to him as he sat, Buddha-like, deep in thought. I was expecting some profound answer but, as the minutes ticked away, I finally broke the silence. "So, what are you thinking about, Lloyd?" "Absolutely nothing," he answered sheepishly, making me laugh at his honesty. After that, given that Lloyd was also the hardworking head of the Yale School of Drama and its Repertory Theater, he trusted me to take on some of the decisions that a director usually makes — the set design, the costumes — and I loved every minute of it.

It seemed like every Black actor in his twenties auditioned for the Dwight Johnson part. Lloyd, much to Tom's frustration and mine, rejected both Denzel Washington (too handsome) and Howard Rollins (because he had played the part off-Broadway). But he finally chose well with Damien Leake, and we began to tape the show at a studio in Hartford. On day two, we were served with an injunction to cease work immediately, courtesy of Mr. Handleman. Tom's older brother, a corporate attorney, quickly studied up on theatrical contracts and worked out a solution with the opposing attorney that anyone with film experience would have laughed at: in exchange for giving Philip a credit as "executive producer of Handleman Productions," he would go away. He immediately accepted. We never heard from him again, but I will be forever grateful to Philip for fanning the flames of a desire that had started in Paris when I was nineteen and had now burst into red-hot flames, buoyed by a line in the *New York Times* review that singled me out after praising Lloyd: "This television production by Joyce Chopra reflects unusual care and thoughtfulness." With that endorsement at my back, how could I not set out with renewed determination to find material that would be my own to direct?

All my instincts told me to stick to a subject I still felt deeply connected to: teenage girls. The documentary I had made, *Girls at 12*, was fresh in my mind, and so much of what I had gone through at that age might enrich whatever story I chose to tell. I thought about a short story by Joyce Carol Oates, *Where Are You Going, Where Have You Been*, which had terrified me when I read it, playing into my worst fear of a stranger coming after my lovely daughter. At the time, I thought that by daring myself to make a film adaptation, I would be putting my hand into that dark well containing my worst fantasies, pull them out into the light of day and see just how ridiculous they were.

But when I reread the story, this time picturing Diane or Mary Anne as the fifteen-year-old whose mother thinks her head is filled "with trashy daydreams," I no longer wanted to just delve into my own fears but also to explore the story's young heroine, Connie, whose dreams of a more exciting life lead her to invite the attentions of a dangerous older man who is pretending to be a teenager, the appropriately named Mr. Friend. After stalking her and learning that that her family is away at a Sunday picnic, Mr. Friend arrives at her house in his souped-up convertible to invite her "for just a little ride." The ending, a duel of wits between the two, inevitably leads to Connie riding off with Mr. Friend in his gold chariot of a car to her probable death in Oates's allegorical, and unfilmable, ending.

Getting up the nerve, I phoned Blanche Gregory, Oates's literary agent, and asked if I could option the screen rights. Both she and the author knew Tom — he and Ms. Oates had been published in the O. Henry Prize Stories collections numerous times — and we settled on a modest sum. When I learned that *American Playhouse's* mission was to help stage directors and documentary filmmakers make their feature debuts, something that was a marvel then and is unheard of now, I sent Lindsay the story with a note saying that Tom would be writing the film adaptation. He readily agreed to support its development.

Those next months collaborating with Tom on the screenplay were among the happiest days of my life. We would spend the mornings together inventing scenes with bits of dialogue, trying to understand the characters' motives, but it would be up to Tom to do the kind of writing that brought it all to life. He would come down from his barn studio with the fully written scenes at the end of the day, often passing Sarah and her friend Cay busy building forts in the woods behind our house, and read them aloud to me. I was always amazed by how he had transformed mere outlines scribbled on 3x5 cards in ways I could never have imagined. The biggest challenge we faced was to turn the Connie in the story, a barely sketched teenager who spends hours painting her toenails and playing her music at ear-splitting volume, much to the annoyance of her mother, into a fully living person. Since there wasn't any description in Oates's story of the town she and her mother lived in, let alone the rest of her family and friends, we had the freedom to invent a world that would make what happened to Connie seem inevitable. Within that invented world, Tom created a restless Connie filled with longing for something wonderful to happen, an adventure that would take her far away from the emptiness of her life.

One aspect we struggled with was how to convey the pain-filled chasm between Connie and her mother without dialogue. As always when writing, Tom had music playing, and James Taylor's sweet voice singing "Handy Man" put him into a sort of reverie. He suddenly imagined Connie dancing to the song in a rapture of her own, unaware that her mother was listening in her own sort of rapture, in a room just one door apart. It happened that James was a friend who lived up the road from us. He dropped by one evening for dinner and, hearing the excitement in our voices about the script, he asked if he could read it. He must have connected to the longing in it because he inquired, very modestly, if he might write our music. James was our first reader, and his request a sanction to continue.

The short story was seventeen pages long, with the last twelve taking place in one scene, outside Connie's house, when Arnold Friend comes calling. The one and only actor I had my heart set on casting as the dangerous stranger was Treat Williams, and I was lucky again that another neighbor had been his high school roommate and agreed to pass along the script. I had seen Treat perform brilliantly as the Pirate King in *Pirates of Penzance* on Broadway and in Milos Foreman's movie adaptation of the musical *Hair,* playing the role of Berger, the leader of the hippie band living in Central Park. Treat was charismatic, even handsome, but there could be something a little off in his eyes, which was perfect for the part. I was excited that he not only lived on Manhattan's Upper West Side but also that he wanted to meet. This would be my first meeting with an actor as a director, and, if I had been given to clammy hands, they would have been soaked. When he opened his apartment door to welcome me, I was taken aback and thought I had pushed the wrong buzzer; the boy before me looked to be about eighteen. I was about to apologize for my mistake and turn away until I peered below his baseball cap and saw the face of a grown man. He was precisely the Arnold I had imagined, but though eager to play the part, he warned that it would have to be on his schedule in late September.

At the same time, I had come under the spell of a remarkable book that also blurred the line between reality and fantasy, *The*

Woman Warrior, by Maxine Hong Kingston. It too was centered on a teenager, this time a first-generation Chinese American girl ironing shirts after school in her family's laundry in Stockton, California, while secretly imagining herself as Fa Mulan, the heroic woman warrior in her mother's tall tales. I sent a copy of the book to Martin Rosen, who had tried to produce our first screenplay, *Joseph's Move*, and who had since become a dear friend. He loved it as much as I did and agreed to finance a deal if I could entice Maxine into giving us a film option. I don't know if it was the success of Tom's play I had produced for PBS or my negotiating the rights to the J. C. Oates story or both, but I was suddenly filled with a sort of bravado, aware that, if I was ever to take my shot at directing fiction films, the time would never be better than this moment.

After speaking with Maxine by phone and hearing the hesitation in her voice, I flew out to Hawaii where she was then living, hoping that if we spoke in person, I could overcome her doubts about optioning the movie rights to a woman who had never directed a feature film before. Maxine radiated intelligence and wit, and the two of us hit it off right away. We even shared the same October birthday. Tom was also smitten with the book, and we both flew out to Stockton to spend time with Maxine and her parents. When her mother learned that there was a bigamist (and possibly a trigamist) uncle in Tom's family, she was delighted and pronounced Tom half-Chinese.

At the end of many months of intense work, we were near completion of not one but two scripts that I had a chance at directing. I thought myself the most fortunate person, especially when the Sundance Institute invited us to attend their month-long June lab along with a dozen other first-time director/writers out in Provo, Utah. We had submitted *The Woman Warrior* in competition, and Tom and I had been accepted. The invitation couldn't have come at a better time; I had much to learn from the experienced directors who would be there, especially about where to place the camera to best tell the story. In the documentaries that I had directed, once I had chosen the people to film, my job was to follow their actions and stay out of their way. I would also be the one to lead the way on choices involving set design, costume, music and props, but there I felt less daunted. Those choices would flow from what I imagined the characters in the scripts would make.

Barely a week after our arrival in Utah, Lindsay sent a message that he had approved our *Where Are You Going* script and would provide half of our budget. The amount *Playhouse* could contribute would have been tiny by Hollywood standards but it was a huge step forward for us, and I spent the evening raising a few glasses with Tom and the aspiring director friends we had just made. As eager as ever to have Treat Williams play the dangerous stranger, I set late September in my mind as a start date for filming, praying that we could somehow raise the rest of the money over the summer. While Tom was enjoying the beautiful Utah mountains and Maxine's company while revising the script with her — she had also been invited along with three actors to rehearse scenes — I was in a state of high anxiety trying to advance the two films at the same time.

I spent the better part of my days rehearsing scenes set in the family's laundry (we had a few props but had to imagine the set), with Mama holding her children spellbound with her Chinese ghost stories. My work directing the actors went smoothly thanks to my time at the Neighborhood Playhouse where I had learned to analyze a scene for its "beats," those moments that alter the dynamics between characters, but, to my great consternation, there weren't enough experienced directors on hand to teach me what I most needed to know about the art of camerawork and where to place the camera to achieve the visions in my head.

When the time finally came to shoot a few of the scenes we had worked on, the space was crammed with observers, and by its end I wanted to crawl under a rock in embarrassment. What I had created was far from what I had envisioned since I'd fallen back on a safe shooting plan consisting of a wide master shot and closer shots of the actors involved. Even as we were filming, I knew that, when cut together, the scene would be emotionally flat, as it had no point of view. I only learned later on and with more experience to ask myself:

"Whose scene is this—meaning through whose eyes is it unfolding?" and then place the camera so it would appear that everything was happening from that perspective.

Afterwards, when friends asked what was the most important thing I had learned out there at Sundance, I had but one response: "Having survived a day with Bob Redford and a few famous directors watching me make a complete fool of myself, it taught me that I just might survive on a real film set when a crew with a hundred eyes looks to me to tell them what to do."

During our breaks, I was continually on the outdoor pay phone trying to reach our New York casting director, hoping that she had found our Connie, a search that was proving far from easy. I learned what the problem was when I asked a few teenage actresses who were at Sundance on other film projects to read the part for us. The girl on the page as they performed her was just so unappealing. In fact, so much so, that I thought the script was a disaster. Treat lightened my mood for a few days when he made a grand entrance by landing his small plane on the lawn and stayed to read the seducer's part with some of the actresses. He was so terrifyingly attractive in his performance that every girl who listened in was smitten and ready to run off with him. But Connie's part still seemed no better.

Tom tried his best to shift my focus away from the torment of casting by reminding me that my other important hire would be our cameraman. Lindsay Law had recommended James Glennon, whose images and use of light in *El Norte* I had much admired, and set up a date for me to meet with him in Los Angeles where he lived. I had been looking at paintings and books of photography to show Jim as a way of communicating the look I was aiming for and found the perfect expression of it in Joel Meyerowitz's luminous collection *Cape Light*. When Tom and I got off the plane at LAX, I immediately rushed to a phone booth to call Jim, the Meyerowitz photo book clutched under my arm, resolving not to work with him if he didn't respond to it. His first words to me were, "Just finished reading the script and you have got to get hold of this fantastic book of photos, *Cape Light . . .* " My immediate response was, "James Glennon, we haven't yet met, but you are hired."

Martin Rosen also visited while we were at Sundance, and I was beyond thankful when he not only agreed to put *The Woman Warrior* on hold but also offered to help us secure additional funding for our new production. Although *American Playhouse* offered to put up six hundred thousand dollars, more than a million was required, even if everyone agreed to work for a fraction of their normal fee. Within weeks, Martin had a commitment from Goldcrest, the London-based company that had financed *Chariots of Fire* and *Watership Down*, the animated feature he had directed, to supply the rest of our budget. It had never occurred to me to film anywhere but the small towns of Connecticut, and I had already scouted for locations there, but Martin had other ideas. Since the budget was so low, and he would be working as the producer without a fee, he asked that we film nearer to his home, north of San Francisco. It was such a reasonable request we couldn't refuse, especially as our locations were ubiquitous, with shopping malls and rundown towns in every state in America. Knowing that Tom's fee as the writer and mine as the director would also be low, and with no other source of income to support us, we rushed to secure a second mortgage on our house to carry us through the coming year. We were taking a big bet that we would be able to repay all of it within five years.

We packed up and went west, moving into a rental house in San Anselmo close to the production office while Sarah, much to her delight, was enrolled as an eighth grader in the local middle school, very glad to be away from the bullying at her old one where she had suffered the misfortune of being given an award as "Top Scholar"; she hadn't yet learned how to either laugh it all off or be tough enough to push back against the teasing that invariably came her way. My own days were filled with driving around, trying to find the house Connie's mother would be forever trying to repair, instinctively knowing that a location told the story as much as the dialogue did, and working with a local casting director to fill out the smaller parts. Mary Kay Place had accepted the mother's role, and we were equally delighted when Levon Helm, the vocalist and drummer extraordinaire from The Band, accepted the father's. I had fallen for him when he tenderly said the words "You are my shining pride" to Loretta Lynn, his much loved daughter played by Sissy Spacek in *Coal Miner's Daughter.*

By now, the art department was busy at work transforming the locations to suit the script, costumes were being fitted, and Treat was due to arrive in ten days to begin filming. But I was near panic as we still hadn't found an actress to play Connie in spite of the efforts of casting directors on both coasts who were on the lookout for her. Facing reality, I told Martin to open negotiations with a perfectly fine young actress I had auditioned weeks earlier who hadn't excited me. It appeared certain we wouldn't find anyone better. I happened to be in the production office when I overheard Martin on the phone with a friend of his, Nancy Ellison, a photographer living on the beach in Malibu Colony, and, while trying to cajole her into taking production stills for free, he lamented about our failure to find our perfect Connie. Whatever she said caused Martin to instantly hand over the phone to me. Without any preamble, Nancy said, "I know her. She's walking past my window right now on the beach." "Who is?" "Bruce Dern's daughter, Laura." Nancy talked as though "Connie" was a real person that existed outside of fiction, a truly strange experience. Nancy was so certain that I instantly knew that our search was over, especially when I phoned Laura in Los Angeles and her answering machine picked up. It was playing James Taylor's recording of "Handy Man."

The next day, I spotted a long-legged teenager with a blonde ponytail cheerfully waving a greeting to me at Burbank Airport, and I liked her immediately. We got into her car and headed to a small studio just a mile away where I planned to videotape her audition to bring back for Tom and Martin to see. A picture postcard of James Dean was glued above her stick shift, the very one described in the script as hanging, blown up, on Connie's bedroom wall. By now, I didn't know what to make of all these coincidences — Laura hadn't even seen the script — and just prayed that I would like her reading. It was more than I could have asked for. In fact, it was quite thrilling sitting in that small studio and witnessing Laura's inner warmth and grace transform dialogue that had seemed leaden coming from other actresses. It was reminiscent of the night when Joan Baez almost knocked me off my chair auditioning at the Club 47. I cast this miracle of a girl on the spot.

I had noticed that she slouched while reading and asked her if it could be corrected. She admitted that, being taller than Treat, she was afraid she wouldn't be offered the role and had thrown her weight onto one hip to lose a few inches in what she called her "scoliosis stance." I assured her that we would take her at any height. A few evenings later, as Tom and I were sitting on our San Anselmo balcony, a taxi pulled up below and Laura unfolded herself, blonde ponytail and all. Tom was so stunned, he could barely trust what he was seeing with his own eyes. "She's perfect," was all he could manage to say.

Although we were working on a shoestring, we didn't lack for talented people to join our crew, especially David Wasco, our production designer, a man so gifted he would continue to shine later on with a variety of films, from *Pulp Fiction* to *La La Land*. I had been gathering art postcards for months and now handed them over to him, including Balthus's erotically charged paintings of pubescent girls that had a dreamlike quality about them. These cards not only conveyed mood but also allowed me to give clear examples of lighting, of shadows desired and the color palette for the costumes and sets. When it came time to film, I could tell that Laura had also taken inspiration from the Balthus paintings by the way she languorously moved in a number of key scenes, while Meyerowitz's book, *Cape Light*, helped David with its photo of a screen door and the hallway beyond in an old house that was uncannily like the image in my head where much of the terrifying encounter between Connie and Arnold Friend takes place.

Since I had never gone to a film school, most of my training in camera placement and lenses had to be on-the-job, and Jim Glennon was the best collaborator I could have wished for. I still had much to learn, and, with time growing ever shorter until the first day of principal photography when I would be facing that crew with a hundred eyes, I was more than a little keyed up. It eased when I sat down to prepare my first shot list with Jim and Tim Marx, my experienced assistant director, a process of thinking in three dimensions about where to place the camera sequentially and deciding in advance whether I wanted it to be moving at any point. I also realized that I could borrow what I had learned in acting classes and had proved useful at Sundance directing the cast: analyze a scene for its beats, those moments that alter the dynamics between characters, and then place the camera where it would be sure to capture them. My stomach remained clenched the first few days of filming, but, as I grew more confident about the technical stuff, from how a dolly move is accomplished to the basics of lighting a room, I began to relax at least some of the time and took particular pleasure in realizing that I had a natural ability to compose a shot that told the unfolding story without the dialogue. I also seemed to have the ability to work well with the cast, knowing how to frame a suggestion for their performance that they would frequently find useful.

Martin was so concerned that I didn't look like a "real" director (that is, male), that, when a representative from the company that was insuring our production showed up, he insisted I yell out, in the most authoritative voice I could summon, "That's a wrap!" after the last shot of the day. Laura laughed since it was only done in movies about making a movie, the rep was impressed, but I found it more than embarrassing and never did it again.

I had hoped to film in order of the scenes as written, but Treat's schedule forced us to film all his scenes with Laura first. These were the most challenging part of the script to stage — two characters verbally dueling for eighteen minutes. Arnold, a rapist, prided himself on his ability to use seductive language, rather than force, to get the girl he wanted. Connie, bored and alone at home, first welcomed the unexpected stranger, stepped outside to flirt a bit, became wary and then retreated into her house, latching a screen door that wasn't offering much protection. In a way, it was a sinister courtship dance, and Treat used his shiny gold convertible almost as a third person in the scene, lying on it, gliding on it, showing off the words he thought witty that he had painted on its sides in his effort to intrigue her, his background as a dancer helping him enormously. Then, just when he couldn't have been more mesmerizing, a scene from his time at Sundance replayed itself.

I had just said "Cut," and I turned to our script supervisor, whose job it was to take notes on the actors' movements, to ask her where Treat's hand had been placed so we could match his position in "take two." The young woman was so transfixed, she had been unable to take her eyes off the snake, and blurted out, "I would go with him, wouldn't you?" Unfortunately, she had stopped taking notes. It's amusing now, but at the time I was furious and almost fired her. Of course, Treat was flattered, and all was forgiven. We had to shoot with his hands in several positions to give the editor options, but it cost time, and, by the end of the week when Treat had to catch a plane, we still hadn't filmed crucial close-ups of Laura standing behind the latched screen door as Arnold tries to "smooth talk" her into opening it. It's a tribute to Laura that, as I read the lines in Treat's place, off-camera, she performed brilliantly. She probably would have done just as well with a lamppost.

Watching dailies each evening was a bit unorthodox since we didn't have enough money to rent a 35mm projector with sound. I didn't care all that much since I knew how the actors had performed, but, this being the days before there were monitors to look at while filming, dailies were my first look at how the scenes had actually turned out. I had set up the shots with Jim Glennon, not just their opening frames but also the direction and speed of the camera moves as well; after that, a third person, the highly skilled "operator," took over. Thanks to Jim, we had Craig Haagensen, a man so finely tuned to the actors that he anticipated their slightest moves and tilted and glided the camera barely a fraction of a second ahead of them.

When I saw the first edit of the film, I thought it was a calamity. All I could see were my mistakes. It was also my first time and a shock to see scenes in public places like diners without background sound although it was I, the director, who had instructed the extras in them to mime their conversations. It had been filmed this way to keep the main dialogue tracks clean so they could be edited without the interference of these added voices. But it contributed to my sense that everything I had shot was phony. But with the addition of "loop group" tracks — actors in a sound studio conversing as though they had been the ones in that diner — and James Taylor's music, I thought it fairly okay until the sound mixer at the Saul Zantz Studio in San Francisco mumbled some disparaging comments as he did his work. Since he had mixed *Apocalypse Now* and *Amadeus,* his reaction to the film was chilling.

With hearts made doubly heavy knowing that Sarah, who had been accepted at Andover, would no longer be living with us, Tom and I packed up and flew back home. My brain knew that it was the right school for her, but it didn't make the parting any easier. It would strain our dwindling savings, but we never hesitated. Then Martin phoned to tell me that he had shown the film to Bob Redford who didn't much like it. It was another stab to the heart.

But the news forced me to think about something Tom said when writing the script: if a scene doesn't alter the world of the story, take it out. It suddenly struck me that the first five minutes of the film were just pretty filler, Connie and her girlfriends arriving at a beach and fooling around, hoping to be seen by some guys. I put up a copy of the film and cued it to start on an ominous wide shot of water at dusk that panned to Connie and her two girlfriends as they wake from a nap on the deserted rocky beach and, in a panic at the late hour, start to run towards the exit road. Their scattered dialogue as they try to hitch a ride lets us know that they were at the beach without parental permission and are afraid of the consequences. If we cut out those first five minutes, it would completely alter the viewing experience because we enter a story that has actually begun, and on a darker note. Dissatisfied as well with the story's title which we used for the film, Tom and I spent hours trying, but failing, to come up with a new one. One evening Helen Cole said, "That terrible man just sweet-talked her out the door." Lightbulbs flashed, bells chimed and we suddenly had our title, except that we changed "sweet" to "smooth" since it was closer to Arnold Friend's style.

With a new title of *Smooth Talk* in place over the recut opening, Martin submitted a print to the Toronto International Film Festival where it was promptly accepted. I flew up the morning of the screening on my own and found my way to a seat way in the back of the theater and on the aisle, ready to make a quick exit when the booing began. My memory of the wave of applause remains overshadowed by a man seeking me out in the lobby and praising the film; it was the director Brian de Palma whose many films I had so admired. I must have blushed as I thanked him, especially when he went on to tell me that I was going to have a big future as a feature film director and needed an agent. Did I have one? To which I responded that the only thing on my mind was to keep myself from being skinned alive. Brian kindly suggested I contact his agent, Marty Bauer, in Los Angeles, adding that he would urge him to represent me if I called. I was barely back home before we heard from the Sundance Film Festival, which Redford had started to showcase independently financed films, and *Smooth Talk* was invited to be in competition.

As with Toronto, I went out to Park City by myself and spent the week not doing very well at concealing how scared I was, saw very few of the other films in competition and spent most of the time walking from one end of the snow-covered town to the other. Only in its third year, there was still an intimate feel to the festival, the swarms of agents and gliterrati not arriving until a few years later after the low-budget *Sex, Lies and Videotape* grossed over forty million dollars. At the closing night awards ceremony, I was so shocked when *Smooth Talk* was announced Best Dramatic Feature that I might as well have been back in grammar school. I tripped going up the few steps to the stage to be handed my award.

Martin was thrilled by the honor, especially as it made the near-impossible task of finding a distributor less daunting. The best deal offered was from Spectra Film, with its promise to open *Smooth Talk* in a dozen large cities and expand out from there. Spectra was smart enough to hire the publicist Peggy Siegal, who knew exactly how to stir up the kind of interest that would bring top critics to a handful of private screenings. Not for all the money in the world would I trade that freezing midnight in February, when Tom, Mary Kay and I waited at a newsstand for a bundle of the *New York Times* to be dropped off by a truck in Times Square, for the ease of reading a review on my laptop in a warm room. Terror turned to joy when we read Vincent Canby's review, especially his grasp of the film's meanings beyond plot.

"In much the same way that Connie evolves from a giggling, supposedly typical teen-ager into a most singular young woman, the film, as it proceeds, gives increasingly clear definition to a very particular kind of contemporary American life. Though Connie is its focal point, 'Smooth Talk' is also about the Wyatt family and what it's like to live in a society that has become one big extended suburb without a 'downtown.' There are shopping malls and movie theaters on highways, but no real center of town, just as the Wyatts have no real center as a family . . . I'm not at all sure that this is what Miss Chopra and Mr. Cole set out to do but, in filling in some of the blanks in Miss Oates's very lean short story, they've drawn a sharp, devastating picture of America at this time. Like the families in the plays of Sam Shepard, the Wyatts are disconnected from their past, though, unlike Mr. Shepard's characters, they aren't haunted by that awareness."

There's no doubt in my mind that Canby's words brought out the long line winding itself around the corner at the 68th Street Playhouse the next day. Our elation was doubled when a friend in Los Angeles read us an equally glowing review from Sheila Benson in the *Los Angeles Times,* who hailed the film as "shiveringly memorable." Then, a few weeks later, the Sunday *New York Times* Arts & Leisure section published Joyce Carol Oates's essay, "Short Story into Film," comparing her story to the film. "Laura Dern is so dazzlingly right as 'my' Connie that I may come to think I modeled the fictitious girl on her, in a way that writers frequently delude themselves about motions of causality." It was startling to read what amounted to her fan letter to us in a big city newspaper, especially since this was the first time we had heard from Joyce since optioning her story. She went on to elaborate on why she doesn't interfere with adaptations of her work. "The writer works in a single dimension, the director works in three. I assume that they are professionals to their fingertips; authorities in their medium as I am an authority (if I am) in mine."

Coney Island's Mermaid Avenue, 1954. *Courtesy of Charles Denson, Coney Island History Project*

Coney Island boardwalk, 1957. *Associated Press image*

Joyce and her
brother David in the
Sea Gate Victory
Garden

Joyce and her father
in a Coney Island
photo arcade

Joyce singing in the
Brandeis Musical
Hey Charlie!

PAULA and JOYCE

Paula Kelley and Joyce at Club 47. *Harvard Crimson*

Joan Baez performing at Club 47. *Photo by Stephan Fenerjian*

Claudia Weill filming Joyce in *Joyce at 34*. *Photo by Honor Moore*

Joyce's mother Tillie interviewing baby Sarah

Tom, Sarah and Joyce

Early members of New Day Films. Top row from left: Amalie Rothschild, Julia Reichert, Jim Klein, Joyce, Claudia Weill; bottom row: Liane Brandon

Joyce at work, editing with Sarah on her lap

Joyce in Nigeria

Nigeria film crew, from left: Nancy Schreiber, Joan Weidman, Debra Franco

Joyce and Jim Glennon on the set of *Smooth Talk*

Film still from *Smooth Talk*, Laura Dern and Treat Williams

Wallace Shawn and Joyce on the set of *Blonde*

Joyce and her BYkids mentee, Jayshree, in India

Sarah and Joyce at a BYkids documentary screening

nine

A FTER THAT, EVERYTHING happened at lightning speed. We were barely settled back home in Kent when I began to receive phone calls from Hollywood, each more improbable than the next. The first was from Steven Spielberg's office setting up a meeting with him, followed by James Brooks himself, the man who had recently won Academy Awards for both writing and directing *Terms of Endearment* as well as the great TV classics *The Mary Tyler Moore Show* and *The Simpsons,* who also wanted to meet soon. Diane Keaton also called, asking if I would consider directing an adaptation of a Larry McMurtry novel she had optioned. I couldn't believe it was actually her, *the* Diane Keaton I admired so much. All this attention from beings I considered almost godlike began to feel like a hallucination. To ground myself, I'd gaze out at the bird feeder at the winter juncos and chickadees flitting back and forth.

The next weeks are a jumble in my memory. I know that I drove down to New York with Sarah, now fourteen and on winter break from her first year at Andover, to meet Diane in her all-white apartment high up in the San Remo overlooking Central Park West and that we sat on white couches next to her enormous white cats and cheerfully talked the afternoon away. I know that Tom and I flew out to Los Angeles, agreed to be represented by Marty Bauer in spite of his greeting us with "So, you want to rock 'n' roll in Hollywood!" because we were so taken with his well-read partner, Peter Benedek. I know I met with a most gracious Spielberg in his vast Navajo-styled office on Universal's lot in Burbank where he expressed his admiration for our film and his hope that we'd be working together soon, took Sarah with me to have lunch with Scott Rudin, then head of production at 20th Century Fox, to discuss the screen adaptation of *Less than Zero* which he wanted me to direct, and listened as Sarah analyzed the novel and explained to him why it wouldn't work as a film, at which point Scott told her to quit high school and come work for him.

I remember being stunned when Jim Brooks showed so much confidence in my abilities that he sent me a copy of the charming screenplay for *Big* to direct while he was trying to get Harrison Ford to star, then telling me a few weeks later that Ford questioned whether I "had enough shots" and turned the film down (it was finally directed by Penny Marshall and starred a far more suitable Tom Hanks). I remember being alone in a hotel room at the Bel Air Hotel on Sunset Boulevard, unable to sleep and begging a doctor for sleeping pills. And meetings and more meetings with studio heads and independent producers until Tom and I finally got together with Jim Brooks at a deli on Pico Boulevard, where we ate smoked fish and celebrated our agreeing to an exclusive contract with his production company, Gracie Films, to develop our next film, a decision I hoped would stop my head from spinning. We had gone from zero to sixty so rapidly that it seemed we had left our real selves behind somewhere in Northwest Connecticut.

Marty Bauer wasn't too happy with our having taken just the one deal, especially as it was exclusive for three years, but we were eager to get back to a more settled life. Brooks's company had a deal with Fox, and its office bungalow was on its sprawling back lot where Tom and I wandered like awestruck kids down the empty New York City street sets we knew so well from dozens of great movies. Before leaving Los Angeles, we talked with Jim about *Joyce at 34* and all agreed that the conflicting demands of mothering and working were far from having been resolved and might be the basis of a romantic comedy. Settled back home, we looked at a slew of the best films in that genre while tossing around professions for our heroine-to-be. Tom came up with the idea of making her a labor arbitrator, using some of his father's more colorful experiences as the labor mediator who had helped settle a strike by New York City's transit workers. It

would take some doing, but we hoped to create a tough female nego-
tiator who used humor and charm to bring warring male factions to
agreement before getting derailed when she finds out she's pregnant.
Once again, I was doing what I enjoyed most: tossing around ideas
for a movie with my husband whose ideas sparked one after another
in me, all in the quiet of our own home.

We hit our first bump when we sent Jim about thirty pages and he
was far from pleased. I was instantly deflated, but Tom grew angry
as he read the notes. As I watched him, it became clear to me that my
husband, who had never worked under anyone's direction before as
a writer, would have a hard time taking anyone's notes, especially if
they were not in tune with his own imagination. I had little experience in handling this kind of conflict and wasn't sure how to proceed;
I badly wanted to work harmoniously with Jim but needed a willing
Tom as my partner. As I anguished over how to soothe Tom, Sarah
unintentionally shifted my focus when she handed me a slim book
she had enjoyed reading, *Bright Lights, Big City*, by Jay McInerney.
The novel was a coming-of-age story, right up my alley, set in 1980s
Manhattan and all wrapped up in a package of cocaine and wit. As
soon as I read it, I saw a movie I'd give anything to make and called
Marty, asking him to find out if the rights were available. Within a
few days, he reported that it had a tangled history — at one point
Tom Cruise had first refusal on the script that McInerney was writing for Columbia Pictures — and after a series of hirings and firings
the book finally landed at United Artists without a producer, and
Sydney Pollack, who had just started his own production company,
took it on even though he didn't much care for the novel.

When Mark Rosenberg, Pollack's much younger partner, heard
that I was inquiring about the property, he immediately wanted to
meet since he loved *Smooth Talk* and, unlike Pollack, was enthusiastic about McInerney's novel. I knew that Marty's partner, Peter
Benedek, represented Michael J. Fox, and I asked him to send
Michael a copy of the novel. He seemed like the least likely actor to
play a coke-addicted *New Yorker* fact checker, but I thought he'd
bring a much-needed humane quality to the part, much as Laura

had done for the problematic teenager in *Smooth Talk*. Michael was excited to be offered the role, and, before I knew it, Michael, Tom and I were sitting on a couch in Sydney's office and agreeing to work together if we could get out of our contract with Jim Brooks and Gracie Films. I asked Marty if it was possible, and he managed to do it all within days. I felt strangely torn, knowing I had just traded away the opportunity to learn from a master writer and director.

The news of my directing a studio feature was made much of in *Variety* and the *Hollywood Reporter* since I was that rare creature, a "woman director," and Michael was at the height of his fame with his *Back to the Future* films. As we sat down to shape a new script — everyone involved thought it best that we begin afresh — Tom and I knew that we were facing some of the same challenges that we had in adapting Oates's short story. Connie was more a type than a person, and McInerney's main character didn't even have a name. The author wrote him in the second person, his novel opening with, "You are not the kind of guy who would be at a place like this at this time in the morning," a stylish choice, quite arresting on the page, but not very helpful in creating a three-dimensional person in a movie. We borrowed heavily from the plot while shifting the tone and I was more than relieved that our producers were enthusiastic about the pages we were sending them. Clearly, this wasn't going to be a repeat of my Jim Brooks/Tom Cole conundrum.

As our first draft was nearing completion, all of Hollywood was suddenly thrown into turmoil. The Directors Guild of America, the most powerful of the film industry's unions, was threatening to go on strike within months if its demands continued to go unmet by the studios. No one could predict how long such a strike would last, and the only way to avoid a production shutdown was to complete filming before the first strike day. I was proud to have recently become a union member, in total sympathy with its demands, but this was a terrible personal blow. By now, Tom and I had our imaginations so completely invested in *Bright Lights,* or, rather, our adaptation of it, that the prospect of the film fading into limbo was dreadful. When Sydney and Mark proposed that we forego the usual prep time and "just go for it," we didn't hesitate, especially as United Artists was so confident in the production they increased the budget so we could film in New York.

Within days and with all expenses paid, Tom and I moved into a small furnished apartment right on Gramercy Park, much appreciating those rare five minutes when we could unlock the gate to the private garden and stroll its paths. Sydney and Mark opened a production office on 57th Street in the Directors Guild building, and I set out to complete the casting. Finding the actress that our putative hero falls for was not going to be easy since Michael was short, and, complicating the issue further, he was lobbying for us to cast Tracy Pollan, an actress he was madly in love with, whom he had met on his hit TV show *Family Ties*. But both producers thought her "too TV" and dismissed the idea, leaving it to me to fudge excuses with Michael that I found truly embarrassing. After that, a stream of young actresses came in to read for the part, from six-foot-tall Uma Thurman to Kyra Sedgwick, but we found none of them "quite right." We finally settled on an attractive unknown with other first-rate actors filling out the secondary roles.

It didn't take long for trouble to break out between Sydney and me. When he heard that I had hired Jim Glennon as my director of photography, he called me into his office to set me straight. "Jimmy's no good. He talks too much. You have to fire him." I couldn't have been more shocked, especially by this new dictatorial tone which I hadn't heard before. He knew perfectly well that as the director it was my right to hire whomever I pleased for that job. It suddenly dawned on me that either Sydney had never seen *Smooth Talk,* for which Jim had received much critical praise, or, if he had, he hadn't much cared for it. Jim, a gregarious Irishman, had been the camera operator on a number of Sydney's films and was regarded by many as the best in the business, but now Pollack was speaking of him as a person of a lesser order, even using the diminutive "Jimmy." That offended me far more than his questioning my judgment, especially as I knew how capable and talented Jim was. I also felt that I owed Jim the opportunity to work on a studio film as his contributions to *Smooth Talk* had been invaluable. If only Sydney had explained his objections in a more collegial way I might have been open to hiring someone else, but apparently that wasn't Sydney's style, and, once over the shock of the insult, I declined. Because of that unfortunate exchange, a chasm opened up between us that would never be bridged. I later understood that, for Sydney, making a film was like going to war, and I was from then on under suspicion of subversion.

Tom was still making changes to the script at the Manhattan production suite, and, now that he and Sydney were thrown so closely together, Sydney wanted to be involved. On far too many afternoons, Sydney would summon me to join them, squeezing the time I needed for planning scenes I would be directing in less than a few weeks. His demanding tone upset me even further, but I didn't have the courage to decline. He had all the power. There were always two female assistants by his side, and every time he suggested a line change the two women would nod their heads vigorously and say, "Yes, yes, that's right, do it," while looking pointedly at Tom, who remained ever polite. But I knew he was seething inside, and we were both astonished that a person as successful as Pollack didn't wince at such sycophantic behavior.

Jim Glennon had his own problems. Being from Los Angeles, he was treated with mistrust by a New York crew that had worked for Sydney many times before and had sensed Sydney's derisive attitude towards him. Since they were the best the city had to offer, Jim had no way to reasonably reject them. My own working days were so packed with the usual decision making that falls to the director — choosing the right locations, the right actors, the right costumes, et cetera — that my brain couldn't slow down at bedtime. For the first time in my life, I developed insomnia, and just when I did manage to fall asleep a car alarm or a police siren would jolt me awake. Somehow, though, in spite of the frost that existed between my producer and myself, land mines were stepped around, and, fueled by the good wishes of friends, Tom and I made it through the first day of filming with the finest bottles of wine waiting for us to imbibe when we crossed the finish line, gifts from every studio head in Hollywood.

Michael was a dream to work with, as was Keifer Sutherland who played his guide to the underground club scene. Unfortunately, the only time we were alone and I could truly feel comfortable was during rehearsals since Sydney hovered over every move I made on the set and arrived each evening to watch the dailies, always sitting a few rows in front of me. He didn't have to say much for me to know from his body language that he was displeased with what he was seeing, and his rare comments only underlined how far apart we were. One of his frequent complaints was that Michael wasn't looking dissolute enough, considering that he was supposed to be snorting coke. He was particularly upset with a scene I had shot in the New York subway. Why wasn't he scratching himself? I replied that scratching wasn't a side effect of snorting coke and would make people laugh as I once did when my mother asked to see my arms when I confessed that I had smoked marijuana.

But Sydney's criticism did shine a bright light on the big elephant in the room — the studio's fear of releasing a film that seemed to celebrate drug use, this being the height of Nancy Reagan's "Just Say No" campaign. I guess that in Sydney's mind — possibly with images from *The Snake Pit* flashing through his brain — the more Michael was blemished and twitchy, the less appealing coke use would be to audiences. Things never got easier, but Jim and I were grateful for the praise we received from the technicians at DuArt Labs who watched what we had shot from the back of the screening room and bided their time, waiting until Pollack had left to talk with us. Oh, how I missed the screening of dailies with my *Smooth Talk* crew.

As we neared the end of the fourth week of shooting, I was beginning to breathe a bit easier and occasionally allowing myself to believe we might be making a good film, especially as Sydney was no longer hovering over my shoulder on the set. He was back at the production office closeted with McInerney and making Tom uneasy. I was far too busy to pay much attention and strategizing with Jim about filming at The Tunnel, New York's then-hottest dance club, situated in a former railroad freight terminal opposite the Hudson River. Jim was working closely with our chief lighting technician,

Dick Quinlan, to keep the lights fairly low for the dramatic effect I was after, much as Jim would do later on when he was the director of photography on the acclaimed HBO series *Deadwood*.

After we wrapped, we rushed to the lab to screen the dailies, feeling rather excited, and found a group of men in suits from United Artists waiting with Sydney. It was the first time they had flown in from Los Angeles and the first time I had actually seen them, or, rather, the backs of their heads. The lights were lowered, the projector began turning and what we saw on screen gave me one of the greatest jolts of my life. Every shot was murky black. It made absolutely no sense, especially as I had seen Jim and Quinlan checking their light meters side-by-side. I was struck dumb as Sydney, looking grimmer than ever, walked out the door, trailed by the even grimmer executives who averted their eyes as if from a mangled corpse.

The assumption was that Jim was guilty, no questions asked. The next day, Sydney called to inform me in his most sepulchral voice, "Joyce, the worst has happened. They want you off the picture." Not one "I'm sorry." I was so upset that I hung up. The phone rang again within minutes, and this time it was Mark Rosenberg telling me how terrible *he* felt and saying hoped to produce my next film to make up for the damage my firing would cause me. I mumbled a thank-you, and we never spoke again. If Mark felt terrible, I was so distraught that I barely ate or slept that night, or the next two or three that followed. A myriad of questions kept whirling in my head. How could the negatives from The Tunnel be so underexposed? Why weren't the producers looking into it? Why had the executives from United Artists shown up just for those dailies and exhibited no trace of surprise when they saw the unusable footage? Had Dick Quinlan, following orders, sabotaged Jim's work? Highly unlikely. But wasn't he also responsible for the lighting, and, if he thought Jim's exposure was dangerously low, shouldn't he have informed me?

Within a day, my firing was big news in the papers. Because much had been made of *Smooth Talk* and of my being among the first females hired to direct a big Hollywood picture, the producers had to go out of their way to publicly discredit me, claiming that

I was behind schedule and over budget. The icing on their cake? Newspapers "leaked" reports that I was guilty of fighting with my crew. It was all laughably untrue, but it was swallowed whole by every studio in town because it so easily fit into the narrative that women were a nasty bunch and never could be trusted to helm a big-budget film. I did call Michael, who had become a good friend, hoping he would stand up for me, knowing that he had been happy working with me those four weeks. Poor guy was torn, but he chose to stay with the production. I learned later on that Sydney and Mark told him that I had been the one against hiring Tracy Pollan and that now that I was gone, the next director would be more than happy to cast her.

Yet the biggest question remained — why had a decision been made to scrap everything I had shot, almost half the film, and start over with a new director? One would think that the executives at United Artists had admired *Smooth Talk,* had looked to Tom and me to create a more filmic version of the novel, much as we had done with the Oates short story, and more importantly, had approved our script before the cameras began to roll. But this was all speculation since I had never once spoken to them, and I now faulted myself for never having tried, happy to leave all the producing to Sydney so I could concentrate on my job of directing. As much as I racked my brain, I really couldn't figure it out. When I heard that they had gone back to Jay McInerney's script I was somewhat surprised, as they had previously rejected it, but again what did I know of the way studio executives think. What I did know was that Sydney had wanted to get rid of me days before filming ever began, and it just took him a while to accomplish the deed.

The press just couldn't let go of the story. Article after article that tracked the film's production status appeared in the papers with identical headlines above the stories: "*Bright Lights, Big City*, the Film Joyce Chopra Was Fired From." And to my eyes it did seem very strange. I wasn't famous, so why bother to attach my name like a Homeric epithet to the film when there was much to say about the well-known director, James Bridges, now at its helm? It appeared that my being fired was not just good copy, it served as a warning to other women as well. "Ladies, beware! Trespassing into our all-male precinct may prove fatal to your health."

Tom and I remained in shock and exhibited it in different ways. He wanted nothing more than to return to the privacy of his study and resume writing fiction, and I wanted nothing more than to have him collaborate with me on a new script immediately to "show the bastards," pure rage gushing through my veins. Each time he resisted my pleas, I became even more frantic. I'm ashamed now of the quarrels I caused that made him so unhappy and our life together almost unbearable for many months. It would take me more than two years to be able to talk about *Bright Lights* without my whole body trembling. We parted company with Marty Bauer and Peter Benedek since Michael was among their A-list clients and they naturally sought to protect him. Peter (who later become the CEO of United Talent Agency) had greatly admired Tom's script, saying it was one of the best he had ever read, and offered to get him studio work, but Tom wasn't in any mood to listen.

Without anyone to guide us, we were now overnight pariahs in Hollywood. Too late, I recalled the advice Irvin Kershner, an experienced Hollywood friend and director of the *The Empire Strikes Back*, had given me when being rushed by Hollywood producers, which I had foolishly ignored: "Don't let them blow smoke up your ass." It was crudely expressed, but now I kicked myself for not paying closer attention to its meaning. I had let myself be seduced by all the attention being showered on me when I should have settled in with Tom at home to write our next screenplay, which we could have tried to produce on our own, independent of the studio system. It wouldn't have been an easy path, but it might have left us feeling whole.

ten

THE LEGENDARY Sam Cohn, one of the world's major talent agents, was on the phone, telling me that he knew we'd been badly treated and that he wanted to represent us. To put it mildly, I was astonished. The man had a client list that ranged from Meryl Streep, Paul Newman and Arthur Miller to Robert Altman, and his reaching out felt like a caress that wiped away the pain. When we met him at the Russian Tea Room in Manhattan where he held court at lunchtime, we had no idea what to expect. He was famous for never returning phone calls and, most strangely, for chewing scraps of paper. Sam was so knowledgeable about music, about literature, he was a pleasure to talk with, and somehow he succeeded in getting Tom back to work on *Castles in the Air*, the script we had begun for James Brooks about a female labor arbitrator, making me close to cheerful for the first time in almost a year.

Then, just as my raw emotions had fairly settled down and our screenplay was progressing, I received news that a *New York Times* film critic, Caryn James, hoped I would agree to be interviewed for an article she was writing for the paper's Sunday magazine about the making of the soon-to-be released *Bright Lights*. Initially reluctant, I finally spoke with Caryn by phone and poured out my grief into her sympathetic ear. I'm not sure what I was expecting her to write, but I hoped for a more honest version of what had transpired. What appeared in print instead was a paean, at my expense, to the director who had replaced me, under the headline, *Bright Lights, Big City: Big Trouble*. It began:

> Murmuring to each other behind the cameras are an unlikely pair of
> middle-aged men — James Bridges, the director of such commercial

hits as *Urban Cowboy* and *The China Syndrome,* and Gordon Willis, the eminent cinematographer on Francis Ford Coppola's *Godfather* films and many Woody Allen movies. Bridges and Willis are methodical and calm, though they have only recently jumped in to rescue this film and are racing to finish before a threatened strike by the Directors Guild of America. Nearby, a production assistant wears a T-shirt with a cryptic symbol on it — an old shoe inside a barred red circle. "There should be a picture of Joyce inside here," he says, referring to Joyce Chopra, the director who began shooting the film and was let go a month later. When the crew started over, they knew that this time there would be no shoe leather — the movie term for filler, usually shots of people walking down the street. Word went out that Chopra's dailies had been nothing but shoe leather, and the film crew's baseball team adopted as their logo the old shoe in the barred red circle.

As I read this, I thought my head would explode. I wanted to sue the *Times.* I wanted to sue Mark and Sydney. The thought of their allowing the crew to wear that logo sickened me. It was as though we had never filmed scenes at the magazine's offices, at restaurants, on night rides through the city, to name just a few locations. Ms. James and the *Times* were giving me my very own lesson in how history is erased and remade by the winners and rather brilliantly fashioned too: if one had to conjure up a scenario of male desire to stomp on a woman in charge, what could be better than that shoe logo with my face under it? And how easily were all the clichés of femininity attached to my apparently small self.

"Chopra, at age 50, looks youthful. She is short and soft-voiced, and as she consulted with Glennon he towered over her. Her husband, Tom Cole, was also on the set. And there, some people thought, were two of her problems. The word was that Chopra relied far too much on Glennon and Cole."

The phrase "the word was" being the last refuge of a lazy reporter, it wasn't too surprising that Tom was reduced to being "the husband on the set" or that I was cast as the "short" female that had to be propped up by my towering male cameraman. And while

I "relied" on Glennon to work out camera moves, Bridges "planned the day's shots with Willis as they drove to the set together each morning." What a difference a verb makes. And never mind that some of the world's greatest film directors, from Fellini to Spielberg, found artistic rapport with a certain cameraman and worked closely with them over and over again. Apparently, I was being told that tradition didn't apply to me.

I wasn't surprised when the film opened to mixed reviews, at best, and was a big money loser for the studio. I can't even say it made me happy. I had never met James Bridges, but he sounded like a kind person, and I was saddened when he died five years later. Nor was I shocked to learn that Mark Rosenberg died within months on a film set in Texas of a heart attack. He was forty-four, an overweight man with an uncontrollable temper who meant well. He had loved our script and if Pollack hadn't undermined us from the very beginning, I think we were well on our way to making a striking-looking film with characters you cared about. Looking back, I do fault myself for not trying to engage Sydney in a more fruitful conversation about what was really troubling him the day he so abruptly demanded that I fire Jim Glennon and I declined. We actually might have arrived at some solutions that would have suited us both, something I learned to do with other producers who had the last word on movies I would direct in the coming years. But those lessons didn't come soon enough to help me with either Sydney Pollack or on my next adventure in the surreal.

It started with Diane Keaton sending me a script, *The Lemon Sisters*, which she had commissioned so that she and her two dearest friends, Carol Kane and the stage actress Kathryn Grody, could all work together, a most laudable impulse. Diane had planned to direct the film as well, but as filming time grew near, she felt that she'd be better off focusing on producing and acting and have someone else take on the directing role. I remember reading the screenplay with great anticipation, stretched out on Helen Cole's couch. I was full of hope that here at last was my ticket out of pariah hell, but, as I read, I became less than convinced. There was much that was charming in the writing, but it edged too often into the sentimental. Then Tom sat down to read it and, knowing how eager I was to be directing again, encouraged me to consider accepting if he did a rewrite, that is, if Diane would be open to it. Diane readily agreed, not entirely happy with the script herself. My most important question, though, before even asking Diane that was, "Can you really let go of directing a script that you worked so hard to develop?" Her response was "No problem."

The story as written revolved around three women who met as kids in Atlantic City and vowed to remain best friends in spite of the travails life might bring their way. When we meet them as grown women, they are performing as a trio, singing at second-rate clubs along the Atlantic City boardwalk. The financing was to come from Lightyear Entertainment, a New York–based company that in turn had secured their money from Miramax. This was one of the first films Harvey and Bob Weinstein were to be involved with as investors after their success as distributors of independently made films. Knowing little about the Weinstein brothers, I went to hear Harvey give a talk about the company at a fund raiser and had to listen to more than an hour of his boasts about the brilliance of his plans, the Academy Awards he would be winning, and the millions that would be flowing into Miramax's pockets. I came away thinking, "That preening jackass is delusional . . . thinks he's going to be the next Jack Warner. I just hope his money doesn't run out before we finish the film."

While Tom was writing away, Diane and I travelled down to Atlantic City to scout locations. Wherever we went, people tripped over themselves to accommodate her. I had witnessed massive crowds of teenage girls clamoring for Michael when we were filming *Bright Lights* on Manhattan streets, but this was something of a different order. It was reverential, as if they were in the presence of a queen. When I returned home to Connecticut, I showed the revised script to a friend, Patrizia von Brandenstein, the production designer of *Amadeus*, in the hope that she would agree to work on a fairly low-budget movie. She loved the Atlantic City setting, and Diane and the producers were as excited as I was to have her on board. Jim Glennon was back at work on another feature so I was pleased that Bobby Byrne, who had filmed everything from *Sixteen Candles* to *Bull Durham,* was hired as our cameraman.

Since the centerpiece of the film was the trio performing, Diane brought in Paul Schaffer, the musical eminence of *The David Letterman Show,* to help create the group's style. Diane and Carol could sing and dance gloriously, and, though Kathryn couldn't quite compete with them in that department, she more than held her own with her warmth and offbeat charm. Things appeared to be rolling along smoothly when Diane suddenly stopped singing and began to scream at Paul. I can't remember what her words were, but if Paul could have slunk under the piano bench at that moment, he would have. Then the moment passed, but no mention was made of Diane's outburst. I came away unnerved and fervently hoping that in future rehearsals nothing would set Diane off again, not that I had a clue as to what had caused it.

With the three actors staying on in New York, the crew and I went down to Atlantic City to prepare. Things seemed to be humming along smoothly when Joe Kelly, Diane's coproducer or, as I was later to dub him, "the Enforcer," asked me into his office. I found him seated behind his desk. "You have to fire Patrizia." "What?" "You have to fire Patrizia." "You're not serious." "Diane is unhappy with her designs." I thought I was hallucinating and back in Sydney Pollack's office. Diane was still in New York and hadn't mentioned a word of her unhappiness to me. Baffled, I reminded Joe that we had all agreed on the designs, that I would be mortified to fire someone who was so talented and who had agreed to cut her usual fee. It was useless to add that she was also the favorite production designer of two film directors that I revered, Mike Nichols and Milos Forman. I left his office, rattled, perplexed, but I did not mention a thing to Patrizia and waited for the next shoe to drop. I didn't have long to wait.

The next day, Joe asked me, once again, to see me in his office. "Diane has lost confidence in you. She'd like you to quit." This time,

I was dumbfounded. It was like being handed divorce papers when you thought you were in a happy marriage. Within seconds, I was back at my own desk and on the phone with Sam Cohn. "I'm in a *Bright Lights* replay, except Diane is hiding behind some thug to do the work for her. I want out. Let them hire someone else." "If you quit after being fired so publicly from *Bright Lights,* you'll never work again. You have to brave it out." I could kick myself now for listening to Mr. Cohn. It was so clear that Diane couldn't really let go of directing her cherished film — no more than Sydney Pollack could tolerate a director with a different style than his own — and that it would take something of a miracle for a good film to come out of this. Patrizia did stay on (I never told her of Diane's wish to fire her), and her sets, not surprisingly, were wonderful, and no more was said about my being asked to quit. But Diane and I could never recover our trust in each other. Although she had loved *Smooth Talk* and pursued me, it appeared easy for her to paper those events over with a new story that suited her present moods. Carol and Kathryn went from being friendly to distant since Diane set the tone and they followed her lead. It felt like I was living in a bad high school drama with a trio of top girls.

The Lemon Sisters was conceived as a romantic comedy, and Diane's part as written — that of a neurotic but lovable woman named Eloise — was ideal for her and one that she had played many times before. Even the costumes she chose were familiar: her trademark wide-shoulder coats, big leather belts that cinched her waist, finished off with black clunky boots. I quickly learned that she was not going to interfere with my camera choices but that she wanted zero input about how she was playing Eloise. With each scene we filmed, I could see her increasingly crossing the line from endearing to the complete opposite. How I wished she would remember how much she had admired my work with the actors in *Smooth Talk* and trust me enough so I could draw her aside and say, "What you are doing is really interesting, but I can only report back to you what I'm seeing in that last take, and it may not be what you intended. Do you want to try it another way?"

Carol Kane's performance was always touching and sometimes hilarious, which almost made up for her keeping us waiting hours for her to come out of her trailer (depriving me of the time I needed for some important shots). Her scene performing "Rawhide" for a then-unknown Nathan Lane as a visiting New York talent agent is the very best in the film. Kathryn Grody remained throughout the loyal and loving friend to Eloise, and Elliott Gould may be the sweetest Atlantic City taffy maker that ever lived, alerting me in between setups that aliens were about to land on the Boardwalk. By the time we finished shooting, I was much in need of a rest, if not an asylum.

It's the rare directors like Martin Scorcese or Clint Eastwood who command the final cut on their films, but I was assured that with my Directors Guild contract, I would be given twelve weeks to deliver my cut without any producer interference; after my time was up, either Diane or the producers had the right to edit the final version. Of course.

I had been praying that when I cut all the scenes together a miracle would happen, that a decent film would emerge and whoever had final cut would want my continuing participation. But that dream was quickly dashed. At the beginning of week thirteen, a screening was arranged for a small invited audience that included the three producers from Lightyear Entertainment as well as Sam Cohn, his always thoughtful fellow agent, Arlene Donovan, and a few of Sam's clients, other directors who happened to be in town. Within minutes, it was painfully obvious that the film was an embarrassment. Sam invited us to all to dine together afterwards at a bistro off Amsterdam Avenue, hoping that as we talked together, some editing solutions might magically appear. The restaurant was an expensive one, and the partners from Lightyear were clearly excited to be dining with the fabled agent. I was feeling so worn down that when midnight had come and gone, I got up to take my leave. I was staying at my friend Honor Moore's apartment in Tribeca, and Tom Kuhn, one of the producers, gallantly offered to walk me to my car parked in the Lincoln Center garage.

It was very cold, and the streets were deserted. Just as we turned the corner onto a windy West 65th Street, Tom Kuhn informed me that, as of now, I was off the film and that Diane would be taking over the editing. I would, of course, still retain the director's credit. He said it all very pleasantly, but the fact that he had waited to tell me until the end of the evening stunned me. At the same moment, I noticed two men dressed in good-looking topcoats walking towards us, and I automatically stiffened. Kuhn and I were now raising our voices in a heated exchange, and when I quickly glanced away from him to see if the men were still coming, I saw that one of them was rushing at us now, holding out a shiny silver revolver and aiming it straight for my neck. "Oh, so that's what a pistol looks like," flashed through my mind. As the gun touched my skin, I instantly flung my shoulder bag to the ground and took off. Behind me, I heard Tom Kuhn saying, "Go ahead, shoot me, I'm not giving you my wallet." It was totally ridiculous, and, to my everlasting disappointment, the guys took off, leaving Tom Kuhn with his money and his manly pride intact. He caught up with me just as I reached the garage, and I realized that, without my bag, I didn't have the money to pay the parking fee. Tom, still pumped from his act of bravery, pulled out a hundred-dollar bill and held it out to me. I had no choice but to take it from his hand.

But my woe didn't end there. When I arrived at Honor's apartment building, it hit me that I was also without the keys and that even if I could get a locksmith I had no way to pay one. It also meant that I couldn't check into a hotel. With nowhere to go, I was ready to collapse on the mat outside my friend's apartment door. I did manage to get in somehow and, reaching Tom, sobbed all my sorrows into the phone. The next morning, I related the post-dinner events to Arlene Donovan, Sam's fellow agent. The fact that the three producers from Lightyear had gorged themselves at dinner at my agent's expense while knowing that they would be firing me that night disgusted her. It turned to farce a few days later. I received a call from Tom Kuhn's secretary telling me, "Tom wants to know when you'll be repaying the money he lent you." I mailed him a check instantly and had to refrain from putting a few choice curses where his name was supposed to be.

The weeks that followed were horrible. I wrote letter after letter to Weinstein, who had now taken charge of the film, with suggestions for repairing it that he didn't bother to answer. I suddenly understood how my Aunt Bessie felt when I chanced to find her weeping in her bedroom when I was just a kid: "Joycie, I'm misable . . . just misable." I was so acutely mortified by a film that had slipped out of my hands before we had even begun filming that all I could think to do now was to take my name off the damn thing. I phoned the Directors Guild for guidance on how to proceed and was told that it was not easy. I would have to submit a written request that showed, in detail, that I had made every effort to contribute to the film's completion but had been rebuffed by the producers at every turn. The thought of appearing, uninvited, at a production meeting turned my stomach, but I knew I had to go through with it.

The first opportunity came when I was notified about a meeting between Diane and a few graphic artists to choose the design of the film's opening titles. When I opened the door to the office, all conversation ceased. Harvey Weinstein in all his glory sat in between Diane and the Enforcer, glowering at me. The meeting resumed, and, following the advice from the DGA, I tried to contribute a thought about typeface. Harvey imperiously cut me off. "Go away, Joyce. No one wants you here." There was absolutely no mistaking what he had said, and, with all eyes on me, I wrote every one of his words down in my notebook, all the while struggling to control the tears that sprang unbidden to the corner of my eyes, the last thing I wished Diane and Harvey to see. I also had to suppress an urge to laugh at the absurdity of it all. How, I wondered, had I so mismanaged my life that someone would actually feel free to talk to me like that? I left, trying to walk with my back as straight as possible, and took to praying that Miramax would just bury the film and put me out of my misery.

As with the stock market, reversals of fortune in the film business are endemic. After poor results at a test screening of Diane's cut of the film, and possibly a taste of the angry outbursts I had been treated to, Weinstein phoned to ask if I would come back into the editing suite and start afresh. He didn't bother to apologize but was civil enough, leaving me unable to claim I wasn't listened to. With his large body jammed beside me, and brother Bob squeezed behind us, we spent weeks trying various solutions in an editing room the size of a closet in the legendary Brill Building on Broadway, once home to the greatest songwriters and music publishers of American pop music.

Mostly we attempted to cut out moments when Diane's performance was too difficult to relate to, but this left us with a film that was way too short. We finally hit on what we hoped was a solution. I had filmed a flashback sequence with an eight-year old Eloise and her girlfriends performing at a Little Miss Atlantic City talent contest for the opening credits and now thought it might be possible to create a back story using the same child actors again. Harvey commissioned a comedy writer to come up with new scenes for the kids and I began scouting locations in Coney Island as a substitute for Atlantic City to save money. I was so excited to be back on my home turf when the day came to begin filming, I headed straight for the ocean, going under the Boardwalk, as the crew measured out dolly tracks for the first shot. I hadn't been there since I was a kid and was marveling at the slanted light coming through the wooden slats overhead, bare feet burrowing in the cool sand, when I heard the sound of heavy breathing. A few yards away in the shadows, a man was leaning against a shuttered concession stand, trousers down, masturbating and leering at me. I dashed for the street, shivering in spite of the sun.

The ending is predictable. The finished film wasn't very good, and, when it was released in the fall of 1989, the critics were not kind. Ironically, Caryn James, in her review in the *New York Times* tried to spare me.

"Among many candidates for the worst scene are the cat outbursts and just about any of Ms. Keaton's reaction shots. She furrows her brow too fiercely, looks too bewildered, tilts her head and once swipes her finger under her nose. Among the other wasted talents is the director, Joyce Chopra, who once made the exquisite, troubling little film *Smooth Talk* and seems to have lost her judgment here."

Caryn's indictment was correct. But I had lost my judgment almost three years earlier when I foolishly thought that I could control a film within the Hollywood studio system. I was alive but had little desire to get behind a camera ever again.

eleven

MORE THAN TWO years passed, and I still hadn't the heart to try my own hand at writing a new screenplay, dream up a new documentary or do much of anything else. Tom was more fortunate. He had just begun adapting a short story that greatly appealed to him for Robert Greenwald, a friend and extremely successful producer and director of MOWs — movies of the week — for all the major networks, with a small studio of his own in a former motel in Culver City. Robert always had at least five projects going at once and had just sold CBS a movie based on a story that was then dominating the news: Pamela Smart, a young schoolteacher in New Hampshire, was on trial for murder after seducing her fifteen-year-old student, Billy Flynn, conspiring with him and a few of his friends to kill her young husband for life insurance money and the chance to be together.

Smart's sensational trial was the first to be broadcast live on American television, with some stations suspending most of their programming to show the proceedings. Having learned from Tom how downcast I was from all I had gone through and wanting to get me back to work, Robert called to inquire if I would direct the film if CBS approved me. The schedule would be very tight since it was now early June and the network wanted to broadcast it at the beginning of their new season in late September. With my mind whirling, I thanked Robert warmly for thinking of me, and asked for a day or two to think it over. With the best of intentions, Robert had just come along and disturbed me more than he could have ever imagined.

Like most directors, the last thing I had ever dreamed of was directing a television movie with lots of commercial breaks. But it

141

wasn't just film directors who disdained working in TV; it was the rare film star who would jeopardize their career by even considering an offer. It might be hard now to imagine the sameness of the TV landscape before 1999 when HBO's *The Sopranos,* a series with the production values of a feature film, changed everything, but until then half-hour sitcoms dominated the airwaves, and movies of the week were on the major networks most Sunday and Wednesday nights. I doubt that I had ever watched a single one. Not surprisingly, of the many thousands produced over the years, only eleven had been directed by women, and one woman had directed five of them. I cringed at the prospect of being in yet another situation where I would be under suspicion for having been born to the wrong sex, especially when I learned that CBS would only approve me if Robert guaranteed that he would take over if I faltered.

Above all, I hated the idea of being away from Sarah for many months at this particular time. After completing her freshman year at Bryn Mawr, one of the few all-women's colleges that were still thriving, she missed co-ed living and decided to transfer to Brown University but couldn't register until the following spring. She opted to spend the fall at a study abroad program in Stockholm prompted by the pleasure she took in cross-country skiing and the sheer beauty of the Nordic landscape. An added attraction was the program's trip to Berlin in early October that, by luck, coincided with the day that East and West Germany were officially reuniting. Tom and I had watched the celebration on our TV, trying in vain to pick Sarah out among the thousands of cheering revelers as they strolled through the Brandenburg Gate.

The following day, Sarah was excited to go on a visit to Sans Souci, Frederick the Great's Baroque Castle in Potsdam. She began to feel unwell by mid-afternoon and had to lie down on the grass, hoping to recover in time for more adventuring. By evening, she was burning up with fever and was so weak that her friends had to half carry her back to their youth hostel. We heard about all of this when she returned to Stockholm and phoned, claiming that she was feeling better and there was no need for her to come home. Back with us just before Christmas, she was happy to show us the few pieces of the Berlin Wall she had snagged, and, though unusually tired, she had gone off to her new life at Brown with real excitement. In a few months, we received her alarming call. "The world is dark before my eyes. I'm afraid to walk down the hall to the bathroom because I'll fall down."

I wanted to bring her home immediately, but she insisted on staying until she completed the semester. When she was finally back with us in late May, her glands were swollen, she had a persistent low-grade fever, aches in all her joints and profound fatigue. Our family doctor tested her for mono, Lyme disease and just about everything else he could think of, but all the tests came back negative. A demeaning label, "yuppie flu," was being attached to these symptoms, with the assumption that the illness was psychological and that the people who reported it were shirkers. It was deeply wounding to Sarah who lay like a limp rag in her bedroom with the shades drawn, since sunlight hurt her eyes. I knew there was no possibility of her returning to college in the fall, and it was painful to accept that there was nothing that either Tom or I could do to alleviate her suffering other than read to her and keep her company. Photos of her and Tom climbing in the Alps the summer before, glowing with health, seemed out of a dream.

Tom could see that I was troubled by not working and, along with Sarah, made a strong case for accepting Robert's offer, assuring me that they would be fine on their own. Although I was feeling uncertain about the project, I phoned Robert back the next day and told him that I would be pleased to accept his offer. I flew out to Los Angeles for what was to become a new phase of my directing career. My first choice for the Pamela Smart role was Helen Hunt, to which the network replied "No way." In spite of her having had the lead in numerous independent films, she wasn't considered a "name." Ironically, this was barely a year before her hit TV series, *Mad about You*, followed by her Oscar win in the comedy *As Good as It Gets*, with Jack Nicholson. But Helen was the only actress I could see in the part, and I anxiously stood in Robert's office as he persuaded the CBS executives that it hardly mattered who starred in the movie since it was the story that would draw the audience. The teenage lover, Billy Flynn, was proving even harder to cast, and, with time running out, our casting director would have to put auditions on tape and send them to North Carolina where I be would be doing the filming.

The city of Wilmington, known as "Hollywood East" or "Wilmywood" by the locals, had excellent production facilities and was located in a state that offered tax rebates to film companies. What made it even more attractive for producers was that it was a right-to-work state, or, more accurately, a no-rights-for-workers state, meaning no unions to insure decent salaries for the local crew. Fortunately, Jim Glennon was available and more than willing to come, truly lifting my spirits. It also helped that we were able to find locations that could plausibly double for a New England town. Before I had left Los Angeles, Helen and I had explored the difficult part she was about to play, and we were daunted, finding it far from easy to see a way into Pamela Smart's emotions. Her story most resembled Barbara Stanwyck's femme fatale in the film, *Double Indemnity*, except Smart's manipulated lover was a naïve teenage boy.

The day Helen arrived on location, ready to dig into her part, we found out that CBS had cast, without consulting either Robert or me, the teen film idol of *Lost Boys,* Cory Haim, to play Billy Flynn. Our hearts sank; Cory was known to have serious problems with substance abuse. I implored Greenwald to do something, but it was too late. The contract had been signed, and Cory was on his way. Our young star arrived in Wilmington late that night, but no one saw him until noon the next day, when he showed up two hours late for rehearsal, barely coherent. Helen was disgusted and walked off the set. Distraught, we phoned Robert together and informed him we would be forced to quit unless CBS found another actor.

Then the incredible happened. The hotel staff woke us early the following morning with the news that Cory had trashed his room and had fled back to Los Angeles. CBS promptly agreed to send us Chad

Allen, an actor who had auditioned on tape. Helen and I instantly took to Chad, and, with a sane producer at my back, the next eighteen days of filming flew by without a hitch. Helen was unnervingly convincing as a narcissistic killer, and Chad was touching as a teenager hopelessly in love with the teacher who had seduced him.

With the shoot over, Helen and I flew back together to Los Angeles with Jim, they to their homes and I to a short-term rental apartment so I could edit the film in a Greenwald editing suite. Although we had shot on 35mm film as was the custom, the negatives had been converted to digital files, and it was to be my first experience with this new method of editing. Gone were the film splicers, the trim barrels, the film cans stacked in racks. It was a marvel to retain multiple versions of scenes, much like our ability with Word documents today, and it helped the work to go almost as fast as our brains. It certainly helped us to deliver the film to CBS within a month. It also helped that Tom and a still ailing Sarah flew out to be with me the last few weeks. It was a real boost to her flagging spirits to have a break from the loneliness of her Connecticut bedroom and get the chance to make friends with the young staff at Greenwald's while she rested on a corner couch in the editing suite.

The morning after the program aired on TV the phone rang shortly after dawn with an unexpected caller, Tom Kuhn. We hadn't spoken since the night he had placed that hundred-dollar bill in my frozen hand outside the Lincoln Center garage so I could retrieve my car. He was excited and couldn't wait to tell me that the overnight ratings for *Murder in New Hampshire* were a staggering "32" or some such number I didn't yet understand. I thanked him as we both pretended that we had parted on the most amiable of terms and I got off the phone as quickly as I could, shaking my head in wonder.

The good reviews the film received acted like a tonic, restoring my zest for making movies. I particularly took pleasure in the *Variety* review praising Helen:

"Ultimately, this parable about children killing children is illuminated by Pamela's schizophrenic acceptance of murder as a reasonable component of life. Reality is made into art by Hunt's brilliantly chilling portrayal, encompassing the adult and the child within her with the unearthly transparency of a phantom."

The head of CBS, Jeff Sagansky, was more than happy, and I was immediately offered another film, with the cringe worthy title *Baby Snatcher*, to be filmed in San Jose. The story wasn't exactly "ripped from the headlines" like the Pamela Smart story, but it did play into every woman's fear of her precious child being kidnapped. I was pleasantly surprised by how good the script was, and it attracted some interesting actors, among them David Duchovny who simply couldn't alter the inflection of a single line of dialogue. I remember thinking, "Poor fellow, he won't have much of a career." Two years later, he landed the lead role in *The X-Files,* playing Mulder, the Oxford-educated FBI special agent who believes in the existence of extraterrestrials. David's flat speaking pattern fit that character to perfection, and, much to my delight, he became an overnight sensation.

That film also had such high ratings that I was now confirmed as a trustworthy *woman* director suitable for television movies about "relationships" and, if a murderous female was involved, so much the better. I wasn't sure I liked that reputation, but the fees I was earning were helping to cover most of our expenses as well as pay off the second mortgage we had taken out to support ourselves when we were making *Smooth Talk.* What followed were a series of television movies with scripts that ranged from decent to quite good, and I simply rolled along with this new kind of existence, living in short-term LA rentals, often with Tom and Sarah, then off to various locations for filming while they returned home. I enjoyed the days spent creating a style for each of the films from scratch and getting all the departments — from costumes to sets — to help me realize them, but it was a lonely sort of life when Tom and Sarah weren't there to hang out with me on the weekends. The new friendships I was forming with actors were intense while we were working together, but in spite of our vows to keep our little bands together, we rarely kept in touch afterwards, with the exception of Laura Dern, who was like my second daughter.

On a Thanksgiving Day as I sat eating a turkey dinner by myself in a near-empty dining room off the El Dorado casino floor in Reno where I had been filming a mystery with Dennis Farina (the most gentlemanly actor playing a gangster I've ever met), I couldn't help but feel a bit sorry for myself. I longed to be home with dear ones as this was a holiday meant for family reunions, but there was not enough time for me to fly to Kent and back. I only half-heartedly toyed with the idea of our moving to Los Angeles permanently, but, curiously, Tom was more open to a big change than I was. His mother Helen had died a few years back, and that, coupled with the pleasure he had taken in the energy of LA before our *Bright Lights* misadventure, made him ready to try life on the West Coast once again. And for a tennis-playing fanatic, outdoor tennis with Norman Lloyd would be available year-round, and hiking just minutes away in the mountains. So, after another round of disjointed living, we acknowledged reality and put our Kent house on the market.

We found a small house covered in bougainvillea to rent in Rustic Canyon, just north of downtown Santa Monica and a few blocks from the beach. We loved telling doubting friends back east that Christopher Isherwood had written *Prater Violet* next door and that many prominent members of the German expatriate community in the 1930s, including Thomas Mann, had lived just blocks away. Sarah was still unwell and still living with us. She had tried going back to college but had to withdraw, once again, partway through the school year. She had been diagnosed with Chronic Fatigue Syndrome, but not one of the doctors she'd seen had been able to help, so she tried Chinese medicine, acupuncture, and meditation, all to no avail. If the devil had asked me to trade my life for her restored health, I would have gladly signed his contract.

Adding to that woe, Tom and I had a blowout quarrel that blew the lid off an arrangement that had been carrying us along quite happily: I so loved Tom's mind and his way of writing that I had been happy to support him while he was doing original work of his own. But, without consulting me, he had agreed to write a screenplay that excited him but that he wouldn't own. It would belong to Sandy

Smolan, a relatively inexperienced producer who had brought him the story. What upset me was that Sandy intended to be the director, and I thought it unlikely that Sandy would ever get the film made as long as he was attached to fill that role. In my mind, I would be supporting Tom while he wasted his talents. It was easy to understood what drew him in. It was the story of Claude Eatherly, the World War II pilot of the reconnaissance plane who gave the all clear to drop the atomic bomb on Hiroshima, then spent the rest of his life tormented by the devastation that followed. Had the deal involved a substantial paycheck that would have allowed me to step back from directing yet another television movie, I might have been more sympathetic. I pleaded with Tom to back out of his contract, but he stubbornly declined, and so our fighting continued until I ungraciously left to direct another TV movie, this one starring Elizabeth Montgomery, star of the '60s sitcom *Bewitched*. None of this was easy on Sarah, who couldn't help but overhear our quarrels, even with her bedroom door shut tight.

When Lizzie and I met, she didn't disappoint; she was every bit as lovable, smart and full of good humor as the character she had played on TV, and I immediately knew we would be friends. She was certainly perfect for the role of the prize-winning journalist, Edna Buchanan, the police beat reporter for the *Miami Herald,* in a script adapted from Buchanan's novel *The Corpse Had a Familiar Face.* What neither of us knew was that she would be dead within the year of liver cancer. What I also hadn't been warned about was that she had a serious addiction — betting on the horses. Many a morning when I visited her trailer before filming, I'd find her on the phone with her bookie getting the lowdown on that day's track conditions. When Lizzie found out that I had never been to a horse race in my life, she invited me to join her that next weekend at the legendary Santa Anita Racetrack. Sitting in clubhouse seats with cocktails and a glorious view of the San Gabriel Mountains, she told me that her grandmother had brought her to the track as a child and schooled her in the finer points of betting. As the horses raced past, I couldn't help but think about our wildly different childhoods: Lizzie hanging around her actor father Robert Montgomery's movie sets with Hollywood stars John Wayne and Bette Davis, while I sat in a darkened Coney Island movie theater gazing up at the same stars in awe. I lost about forty dollars that day but had a wonderful time.

When the movie aired, it did so well that CBS immediately ordered another Edna Buchanan mystery. Once again, I moved into a high-rise hotel in downtown San Diego, which we were substituting for Miami. I was awakened in the middle of the night by the sound of hangers rattling in the closet. Then the room, actually the entire hotel building, began to sway back and forth, which terrified me as I was on the twentieth floor. I crawled from the bed towards the phone when the swaying finally stopped, but the line was dead and the electricity off. It took hours to learn that I had been feeling the aftershocks of a huge earthquake in Los Angeles 150 miles north. The relief I felt when I finally reached Tom and Sarah was immense, as was their relief that they had survived the shake. They both had huddled in separate doorways as objects all around them flew from shelves and tables. Except for the chimney falling off, our house and all the houses on our side of the street were barely damaged, but just a hundred feet on the opposite side it was all rubble.

But as the saying goes, the show needed to go on, and, when filming began, I made my usual early-morning visits to the principal actors while they were getting their makeup done to see if they had any questions or complaints. I knocked on Lizzie's trailer door, and this time it took her longer than usual to open it. She was feeling "just a little off, but not to worry," she assured me, "it's only hemorrhoids." I immediately told Jim Glennon, whose brow furrowed. "You know, I've been having trouble lighting Lizzie's face. It's changed in just six months, more yellowish."

Lizzie and I never spoke about it again, and she pushed on, never complaining and always the first to arrive on set, cheerily greeting the crew. Our last day was brutal, going well into the night, but, in spite of the pouring rain, Elizabeth Montgomery finished her job. The next day she checked herself into Cedars Sinai Hospital, and she died eight weeks later from cancer that had spread from her colon to her liver. Everyone who knew her was in a state of shock. She had just turned sixty-two the month before.

twelve

I WAS LIVING IN Los Angeles, the heart of the moviemaking world, but I wasn't making the kind of films that I would want to see. I had enjoyed working on the TV films, often with fine actors, and even had the opportunity to direct a short-lived series, *Angel Falls*, starring the alluring Kim Cattrall, but none of the scriptwriters of these films had been free to create truly complex characters since commercial television had to appeal to the widest audience possible. It had now been more than ten years since I had worked on a script of my own, and I was restless to try again. I had little desire to reach out to any of the broadcast channels but rather preferred trying one of the new commercial-free cable networks that were coming up with innovative programs.

My mind scanned all the short stories and novels I loved with a female as their central character that seemed suitable for adaptation. If it was in the public domain and I wouldn't have to pay the author, all the better. When I suggested *Sister Carrie* to Tom, Theodore Dreiser's classic story about greed and lust, he became just as intrigued as I was with its story about Carrie Meeber, a naïve but spirited country girl who arrives penniless in the Chicago of the 1890s with hopes of acquiring the finer things in life. Exposed to the rapaciousness of capitalism at its worst, our heroine fights her way through the only way available to her: exchanging sex for money, eventually achieving her independence as a stage actress in New York. It would be a perfect role for Laura Dern. With a proposal in hand, we turned to Robert Greenwald who was able to arrange a development deal for us with Allen Sabinson, the head of production at the A&E cable network. I was as excited as I would have been if we were writing a movie script for a thousand theaters. All that mattered was working, once again, on a film that I was passionate about.

I threw myself into researching the period and became just as fascinated by the novel's troubled publication history. With his massive manuscript completed in 1899, Dreiser submitted the work to Doubleday where it captured the attention of an editor, Frank Norris, who offered him a contract for publication. Unfortunately, Mr. Doubleday's wife read the book and decided that it was thoroughly scandalous — how could her husband even consider publishing a novel about a fallen woman who not only remains unpunished for her sins but also is rewarded with success at the end of the story. Her outrage led to a struggle between Dreiser and Mr. Doubleday, with the author demanding that his publisher fulfill his contract. Acting on his lawyer's advice, Doubleday did precisely that by printing only a thousand copies of the book and refusing to distribute them. With no one to promote its sale, only 456 copies were sold. Dreiser had a nervous breakdown and didn't write another book for ten years, a reaction I could sympathize with.

With the approval of Tom's third draft at A&E, we headed into pre-production and began to work on budgets. I was all set to fly to Chicago with our art director to scout locations (as usual, a collection of postcards and paintings, this time of nineteenth century Chicago, in my backpack) when Greenwald phoned with the news that the network had suddenly changed owners and that Allen had been instructed to drop everything in development. Boom! With those few words, all my hopes of making something I could really be proud of went up in smoke; it was so awfully reminiscent of the day Martin Rosen informed us that Selznick and Brown had been fired as heads of production at Fox and that *Joseph's Move* was not going to be made. No matter how many times this happened, the pain was just as acute. I found it even harder to bear that all of Tom's fine work on the script would be shelved, knowing that, if not for my enticing him, he might have stuck to his play and fiction writing where the chances of his work being seen would have been far more certain.

Tom was now pressing me to move back east. He missed his siblings and his Connecticut friends, especially Arthur Miller, far more than he had imagined he would when he embraced the move to LA. We had often dined with Arthur and his wife, the photographer Inge Morath, at their Roxbury home in the past, and he and Tom had grown particularly close. The letters they had been exchanging, which veered from the political to the personal to the wryly humorous, made Tom eager to be living near him again and resume their daily walks. I had mixed feelings; it was so much more convenient to be living in the city where I edited the movies I directed, and the year-round warm weather was so very comfortable. On the minus side, it had grown increasingly poisonous to live in a company town where you are constantly aware of who is higher on the ladder of success than you are. No matter how many TV films I directed with high ratings, it was clear that I was never going to break into that clique of white males who directed miniseries and the "classier" *Hallmark Hall of Fame* specials.

What really swayed me was Sarah's decision to attend graduate school in New York. During our time in Los Angeles her health had taken a leap forward, and she had returned to school, going back to Bryn Mawr to double-major in British literature and history, inspired by all the reading she had been doing on her own. She was about to graduate summa cum laude and had been awarded fellowships from a number of English departments across the country. I had secretly hoped she would take the one from UCLA, tipping the scale to our remaining in Los Angeles, but when the Columbia University offer arrived, and with it the prospect of living in Manhattan, there was no question about what she'd do and what I would do. We had been separated by a continent for more than two years, and I didn't much like the prospect of that separation continuing in the years ahead.

To celebrate our decision, Tom and Sarah cooked up a three-week father-daughter trip to Germany (a play of Tom's was in production there) while I busied myself prepping a TV movie that my agent, Paul Alan Smith, hoped I wouldn't agree to direct about high-end call girls, with a title that tells the story: *L.A. Johns*. It was trashy, but I enjoyed every moment of it since I got to work with someone I was a big fan of — Debbie Harry of the rock band Blondie, who got to play the madam. So many of the band's hit songs — "Heart of Glass," "Call Me" — would have made a perfect soundtrack for the film, but we couldn't afford the licensing fees. Fortunately, it was the rare film shooting in LA, so I was able to be on hand when Tom and Sarah's plane was scheduled to bring them back home. As soon as they stepped into view I could see that something was seriously amiss; Tom looked as though he had aged thirty years. At first, I thought it was just a bad flu, but, when his temperature suddenly spiked to 105 degrees the next evening, Sarah and I became so worried we rushed him to a nearby hospital where a doctor told us told that he was severely dehydrated and they would have to keep him overnight. That overnight extended into days.

After various tests and consultation with an infectious disease specialist who checked a list of possible outbreaks in Europe, no explanation could be found. The high fever persisted for almost a week, and, as the nurses packed poor Tom in ice from head to toe in an attempt to bring it down, I began to shiver in sympathy and had to leave the room. The fever finally broke, and he recovered enough to leave the hospital but was so weak he was barely able to lift his arms. With no choice but to go through with the move since our lease was about to expire, I boxed everything up with Sarah's help and placed it all in storage. We would now be relying on friends to put us up until we found a place of our own.

It didn't take long to find a small bungalow to rent in Washington, Connecticut, near old friends, and we settled in with enough borrowed furniture to live comfortably for a while. Tom was still in no condition to write, and it seemed more than likely he would never recover his clarity and strength. But that wasn't all that was distressing. Our situation was becoming financially precarious; in addition to our usual living expenses, we had used credit cards to pay for the last two years of Sarah's college, and it was becoming increasingly difficult to keep up with the payments. I had a hard time focusing much on anything else, and I couldn't help but brood for hours, imagining what my life would have been like if I had never quit my well-paying job at WGBH years earlier instead of rushing blindly into the life of a freelance artist. I never would have experienced the highs of making *Joyce at 34* or *Smooth Talk*, but it would have spared me these painful lows. More worrisome, I had just turned sixty-two and had never once given any thought to how I would support myself as I got older, nor had Tom. If he had stayed on at MIT as his father had beseeched him to do, he would by now have a substantial retirement plan with half of Sarah's college education paid for.

I decided to to seek advice from our friend and accountant of many years Richard Koenigsberg and could barely keep myself from bursting into tears the second I began my tale of woe. After offering me some kind words, Richard placed a phone call which at first I assumed was related to some business of his own, saying very few words other than the occasional, "I see," or "Uh-huh." After hanging up, he looked at me and grinned, "Did you know that you have a supplemental pension plan funded by producers' contributions at the Directors Guild and there's over one hundred thousand dollars in it which is yours for the taking?" I was speechless.

Good fortune followed good fortune. Allen Sabinson, still head of programming at A&E, called soon after to talk about a film they were developing and asked if I would be interested in directing it. I could have kissed him, especially when he told me who was involved. Gene Wilder had written a murder mystery that he would star in, and Allen thought we would work well together, particularly as he lived only an hour away in Stamford. Setting his story in Connecticut in the late 1930s, Wilder had created a retired theater director who had so many hits on Broadway he had been nicknamed Cash. Not unlike, Miss Marple, Cash Carter was a consulting detective for the local police chief who valued the special abilities that made him such a successful theater director — an understanding of people's motivation and his close observation of seemingly unimportant details.

The catch was that Gene had to approve me, and I was to initiate the first call. I embarrassed myself in the first few minutes when, after praising the script, I asked him if this was the first one he had written. "Well . . . I did write *Young Frankenstein* and a few others." Why he overlooked my gaffe I'll never know, but he invited me to meet a few days later at the old country house that Gilda Radner had left him when she died. Any apprehension I had about meeting an actor who I was in awe of disappeared within minutes. The half-hysterical character that he often played was just that, a character he played. He was far more like the unruffled, Zen-like Waco Kid in *Blazing Saddles,* Mel Brooks's spoof of traditional Westerns. But his eyes were indeed bright blue and his hair a mess of curls.

Many of New York's best stage actresses were eager to play his girlfriend Mimi, but Gene's heart was set on the one and only Cherry Jones. When Cherry came to our casting director's office on 57th Street just to meet, I sat quietly by as the two just beamed at each other and didn't stop until the shoot was over. But his other great wish was denied him. Gene had hoped that he could sleep in his own bed in Stamford while filming, just as he been able to sleep in his Bel Air house when he worked in Los Angeles. Unfortunately, that hope dimmed as soon as a budget was prepared. We were too far from Manhattan for a crew to travel daily, and housing them in Stamford would have been prohibitively expensive. Toronto was chosen for its variety of locations, its favorable dollar exchange and its profusion of good actors to fill the secondary parts.

Although he had directed four features himself, Gene never once looked over my shoulder. He was perfectly happy to stick to his role as an actor, and the producer that A&E had hired, Fred Berner, amiably stuck to his job as well, staying well out of mine and always finding ways to stretch the budget to allow for the best period costumes and furniture. Added to this was the pleasure of collaborating with Bruce Surtees, who came on as our cameraman. Known as "the Prince of Darkness" for his muted style of lighting, Bruce had shot everything from *Dirty Harry* to *Risky Business* and *Beverly Hills Cop.* Although I missed being home, I loved being out of town on this particular shoot since it allowed me to dine every Saturday night with Bruce, Gene and his new wife, Karen, soaking up Bruce's stories of working with Clint Eastwood and Gene's stories of working with Mel Brooks, accompanied by glasses of Sancerre, Gene's favorite wine.

It happened that a week before I left for Toronto, I went out with a real estate agent who was quite excited to show me an old farmhouse that was about to come on the market in nearby Roxbury, exactly the kind of place we had been searching for now that a down payment could come from my Directors Guild windfall. But when she referred to it as "The Marilyn Monroe House," I immediately said "No, thanks." Any thought that we might be perceived as wanting to own part of Arthur Miller's past life made me uneasy. I vaguely knew that he had purchased a small house with money he made from his first successful Broadway play, *All My Sons*, and had used it as a weekend retreat with his first wife, Mary Slattery, and their two young children. Following their divorce, he lived there with Marilyn until they were forced to move a mile away because the house sat right on the road, with no real privacy.

Predictably, after looking at other houses for the rest of the afternoon, which were either too expensive or too ugly, I became downhearted. "You're sure you don't want to take a quick look at the Monroe house? You don't even have to go in." The property she drove me to consisted of four acres and a white wooden farmhouse dating from 1810, surrounded by land that had been given to the town's land trust and would never be built on. *Not particularly amazing, but pleasant enough* was my first thought. My indifference turned to joy the minute I walked into a living room floating in sunlight, with floor-to-ceiling bookcases lining the entire length of the room opposite the windows. There was something about the place that made me want to stay there forever. "I know there are bedrooms and a kitchen, but I don't have to see them to know we're going to buy this place."

Luckily, Sarah was up from Columbia for the weekend, and she and Tom came right over. They fell in love as quickly as I did, and it was left to Tom to work out the purchase as I flew up to Toronto and *Murder in a Small Town*. Eight weeks later, on our last day of filming, I mentioned to Gene that all our stored furniture had arrived in our new home and Tom was getting everything ready for my return. Gene looked solemnly at me with his big blue eyes, took my hand and offered brotherly advice. "Now Joycie, he's probably arranged the furniture in ways you won't like, but don't say anything for three days, then maybe you can move things around bit by bit." Sorry to say, I didn't last even one night and confessed my crime to Gene, adding that, although Tom didn't have strong feelings about where a couch or lamp was placed, when it came to everything else in our life together and I got too bossy, he sharply reminded me, "You are not *my* director."

It was only after we purchased the house that we learned something about the property that thrilled us; the little shack on top of a knoll was where Arthur wrote two of his most famous plays, *Death of a Salesman* and *The Crucible*. Not only that, he had built it with his own two hands. The agent who sold it to us never mentioned it, stressing instead the house's Monroe connection. Arthur hadn't been there in almost fifty years, and when he came to visit he was overjoyed to see it still standing and in good shape. It's not too surprising that it took Tom months before he felt comfortable sitting down at the wooden door that Arthur had used for a desk and begin to do his own writing. His own health had improved somewhat, and when he wasn't up in the shack, he took to clearing out much of the land that had been overgrown with vines from long neglect. I got ambitious and planted my first perennial flower garden, and Tom cheered me on when the peonies and foxgloves bloomed. For the first time in a life of moving from one film location to the next, I began to feel a real connection to where I lived and had little desire to go anywhere, which was upsetting since I knew staying home for long wasn't really an option. I needed to continue the flow of income.

When the Disney Channel inquired if I would be open to directing *Rip Girls*, a film about surfing, I was incredulous; I was the last person in the world suited for the job. Although I was fairly adept by now at filming car chases and gunfights, I knew that the surfing part of the script would be way beyond my knowledge. But . . .

if the producers at Disney were okay with my on-the-job training, I thought it might be exciting to learn yet another aspect of film-making. I also liked the script. The story revolved around an over-protected young girl from Chicago who suddenly inherits valuable beach property on one of the Hawaiian Islands from her deceased mother's family and, despite the protests of a father and stepmother who would sooner have her sell it for millions to a resort developer, she discovers her Hawaiian roots and a love of surfing. In the end, right-thinking girl that she is, she decides to donate it all to a nature preserve.

On my way to the shooting location on the Gold Coast in Northern Australia, which would substitute for Hawaii — without unions it was less expensive to film there than in the States — I stopped off in Los Angeles to meet with the Disney executives and cast the lead parts. After parking my rental car on the studio lot in Burbank, I found my way down Mickey Mouse Avenue to the Team Disney executive building that was hard to miss, having the distinction of ten-foot-tall statues of the Seven Dwarves circling its rooftop. I had never been in such a seamless corporate setting; every object on every desk bore the Disney logo. I was given an indoctrination in the Disney style which, not too surprisingly, required using bright colors whenever possible, and one specific requirement for this film that must have been conceived in the 1950s: the female surfers' two-piece swim suits would have to cover their belly buttons. (That almost caused an insurrection later on from the champion teenage surfers we flew in from Hawaii.) When I left Burbank to set out on my new adventure, I had a new Mickey Mouse watch strapped to my wrist for good luck.

After landing in Brisbane and arriving at the hotel chosen by the producer about two hours south of the city, it took but a quick glance around to see that I would be spending the next two months in a most demoralizing place. Instead of being on the coast, we were a mile inland in the middle of a wide one-street town with barely a pedestrian, tree or shrub in sight. If only it was still unpaved and muddy with horses and cowboys I would have able to locate myself, but standing there with the sun's haze blurring my vision, I wanted nothing more than to start running. Fortunately, there was the usual location scouting job to ground me, and after driving along the gorgeous coast for a few days I felt considerably better, especially after finding a secluded cove that seemed ideal for our story, with waves that would challenge the experienced surfers yet not be too daunting for our heroine to attempt to ride.

I was also cheered when "living legend" surf cameramen George Greenough of *The Endless Summer* fame agreed to teach me about filming in the waves as well as direct our second-unit water photography. George quickly helped me realize how impossible it would be to shoot scenes with dialogue while the kids were sitting on their boards, waiting for the next wave. Never mind the sounds of the surf and wind obliterating speech, nothing stood still out there. You could plan on a shot but, by the time you turned your camera on, the actors would have floated yards away. When I asked how these kind of scenes has been filmed in previous surf movies, George had me look at a few and I quickly realized that they had all been shot in a studio tank, looking down on the actors, or used CGI (computer-generated imagery) to replace the tank's walls with white clouds and a blue horizon, a technique I would later learn to use when I had to make it look like the Hollywood Hills were on fire.

This would also be my first experience working with an Australian crew, and, except for the script supervisor, it was all-male, unlike most of my American-based crews, where I had worked with female production designers, costumers, assistant directors and others. It was led by David Eggby, the man who had shot the original *Mad Max* movie, and though David had been the cameraman on over twenty-five films, this would be his first time working with a woman director. Considering all the extra challenges I had to deal with (the cliff leading down to the cove was treacherous; the line producer was fired for incompetence, and I had to take on his job as well), it was a relief that David and I were getting on amiably, that is until a sudden afternoon storm forced me to quickly rethink a shooting plan. I huddled with him on the windblown beach, inviting suggestions. David offered up one that at first seemed fine until I realized it wouldn't quite serve the script and went with an altered plan of my own. From that moment on, David treated me as his enemy number one — I was a female that had rejected his plan in front of the guys. Overnight, the entire crew went from a cheery "Hi, mate" to turning their backs. If I found my job difficult before, with this new test of wills it became emotionally exhausting. On the last day, I confess that I took delight in David's shock when I handed him a thank-you present in the hotel elevator, my custom with key crew members at the end of a shoot, then flew back to Los Angeles to edit, hoping that I would never have to see him again. It didn't quite work out that way.

It started with Joyce Carol Oates coming back into my life the following year. I had just finished reading her novel *Blonde*, a somewhat fantastical portrayal of Marilyn Monroe's deeply troubled life, when Greenwald contacted me with the news that he had optioned the book and was going to produce it for CBS as a miniseries. When he asked me to direct, my initial impulse was to immediately say "Yes, absolutely!" since I had so admired the novel. It would also be my first opportunity to direct a miniseries, a step up that I had never thought would come my way. What held me back was Oates's unflattering portrayals of Arthur Miller and Richard Widmark, another of my Roxbury neighbors, who had once starred opposite Marilyn in a thriller. I knew Dick as a considerate neighbor, a man I had always had a big crush on, but in Oates's fictional world, he was portrayed as a sexual predator. As I was worrying about all this, bent down on my hands and knees weeding my flowerbed to calm my brain down, I heard a voice boom out, "Joyce, how the hell are you?" Dick had stopped by in his powder blue convertible to say hello, warm and friendly as ever. I already felt so guilty that I could barely get out a reply. All I could see was the fictional Dick hovering inches behind him.

In the end, my desire to direct the miniseries won out, though my unease didn't really go away. I decided not to mention it to Arthur or Dick and, assured that Tom would be fine without me, flew off once again to Australia. I initially thought that Greenwald had made the wrong decision when choosing Melbourne as our filming location until I arrived and realized that this vibrant city was far better for our miniseries than Los Angeles; it still had grand old movie palaces and "period correct" buildings that only needed our actors to bring them to life. CBS allowed us to cast a new and talented actor, Poppy Montgomery, as Marilyn, since the rest of the principal cast was so well known: Ann-Margret, Patrick Dempsey, Kirstie Alley, Eric Bogosian and my favorite, Wally Shawn, who was to play Marilyn's agent.

As always, the choice of cinematographer was a major decision, and I was taken aback when our production manager, Gina, asked if I would agree to meet with the very same David Eggby who had behaved so abysmally just months before. Working as the cinematographer on *Blonde* was a plum job, and, with his resume, he had every reason to hope that he would be hired. It must have been a blow to him when he learned that I was the director. Although I told Gina it was absolutely out of the question, she kept imploring me on her old buddy's behalf, so I finally agreed to meet for a quick coffee, puzzling my American producer who knew about the hard time Eggby had given me. "Why are you even bothering?" "Curiosity," I confessed.

When we met, David was duly penitent and kept repeating how ashamed he was of his past behavior. I was expecting him to acknowledge how hard it had been for him to work with a female director for the first time, but he never came close to the topic. I felt sorry for him because he probably needed the work, but I was unmoved. It was an immense relief that Jim Glennon, who had just come off filming Alexander Payne's dark comedy *Election,* was free. Neither of us ever had any complaints about our Australian film crew in all the weeks of filming. It was actually the crew that had reason to complain about us: we Americans didn't know how to take it easy, and they were right. They refused to work the long hours we were used to and at double their normal speed.

Tom flew out west to stay with me while I settled into editing at Greenwald's Culver City studio just days before the 2000 presidential election. There was a big TV in back of the room where we were working, and I had a hard time not looking at it; the drama of Florida's hanging chads had begun. The image of the Republican protesters who had been flown down to bang nonstop on the election office's windows will remain indelibly marked on my brain. The election also brought a painful rupture in my deep friendship with Jim Glennon. By now, he had been cameraman on almost a dozen of my films, but we had never really talked about politics. Assuming we shared the same opinions about the role of government since we were of like mind about art, I forwarded him a liberal op-ed piece a few days after the Supreme Court decided the election in favor of Bush. His reply was filled with scorn verging on rage. Within a week, we went from being so close I used to joke that our brains were touching, to finding each other intolerably stupid. We agreed it was better not to speak or e-mail at all until we both cooled off.

Blonde was broadcast on two consecutive Sunday nights and greeted with almost universally poor reviews. Or, rather, the films were panned, and Poppy Montgomery received raves. I was happy for her, but I was crushed. And instead of this being the first of the many miniseries I hoped to direct, it turned out to be my last. But I wasn't the only one to suffer a career setback. Suddenly the era of Wednesday and Sunday Night TV movies was over. Reality TV had exploded onto the scene with *Survivor* and *The Bachelor,* and the thrill of the contest brought huge audiences to the flagging networks at far less cost than producing films. Not only was I out of a job, so were the thousands of grips, gaffers, food caterers, drivers and extras that had contributed their skills to over two hundred movies a year.

thirteen

I T CAME AS a surprise when the Hallmark Channel offered me
The Last Cowboy to direct. Knowing how scarce directing jobs
were, the producer felt no shame in bargaining my fee down by 50
percent, and I knew I had no choice but to accept his offer if my aim
was to keep working. The film was set in Texas, and Jenny Garth
had been cast to play a horse trainer who returns to the family's
bankrupt ranch to claim her inheritance and battle with her father
about the ranch's future; an unknown Bradley Cooper was cast to
play her love interest. On my last day of filming a cattle drive, my cell
phone rang with an urgent request from our family doctor. "Mrs.
Cole, could you please urge Tom to return my call? I've already left
him more than a few messages," "Can't you tell me what this is
about?" "I'm sorry, I have to speak to the patient himself."

Tom had been to the doctor's office for his routine yearly physical earlier in the week and it struck me as odd that he hadn't spoken with the doctor about the results. Clearly something was amiss.
When Tom finally connected, the news was worse than either of us
could have imagined. His blood tests showed that he had multiple
myeloma, a cancer of the plasma cells in his bone marrow. Neither
of us had heard of the disease, and when we rushed to our separate
computers to research articles about it we were both petrified; life
expectancy was about a year and a half at best.

Sure that the guillotine was about to drop, Tom didn't waste a
second; he made an appointment to start chemo at a nearby hospital
almost immediately. I was on the next plane home that night, trying my best to tamp down my own panic, especially after he told me
about the plans he had made. I urged him not to rush into treatment

before consulting with our friend, Paul Marx, a senior physician at Sloan Kettering in New York, sure that our local cancer center might not have the most up-to-date treatments available. To my immense relief, Tom listened, and, when contacted, Paul sprang into action and was able to get him an immediate appointment with one of the best myeloma specialists in the country. Ray Comenzo was a perfect match, caring and a lover of books, who assured Tom that new treatments were coming along that might give him more years, perhaps as many as three or four, which suddenly seemed a lifetime to both of us.

Our biggest hope was the possibility of a stem cell transplant. The odds were high that either Tom's siblings' or Sarah's blood might be a match with his own. If that happened, the cells taken from their cancer-free blood and transplanted into Tom's would bring about a remission that had a real chance of lasting. Alas, to our great disappointment, none matched. Knowing how difficult the news was, Comenzo proposed a different treatment plan; once the course of chemo Tom was now taking made him as cancer-free as possible, the lab would harvest his own stem cells, freeze them and, after blasting his body with a final high dose of chemo to kill any lingering myeloma cells, inject the harvested stem cells back into his body. Once there, they would grow into new healthy blood cells, but at the terrible price of weeks of debilitating side effects. Tom was more than willing to pay the price. I never once believed that my dear husband would die, sure that his death sentence would somehow be commuted. Perhaps that denial helped me to remain fairly calm throughout his illness, the best thing I could have done for him.

It's strange how quickly one adapts to a life of hospital visits. We were so grateful for the time in-between the chemo drips. Tom tried as much as possible to keep up with his writing life, and I busied myself around the house and garden until the weather turned cold. Arthur Miller was the most faithful of friends, calling Tom most days to buck up his spirits. Sarah returned home from Columbia late spring, and it was a pleasure to have a young person around the house. I was now more than eager to find work in New York so that I could stay close to Tom.

My agent, Paul Alan, suggested I try my hand at directing episodic television, the only genre I hadn't yet worked in, but I was doubtful. Most TV shows on the three major networks continued to be either crime procedurals or sitcoms, and I couldn't see how I would fit in even if they would have me. The episodes were already cast, costumes and sets fixed, and the producer/writer ran everything. Directors were hired for individual episodes with very little for them to direct except the camera set-ups and the actors brought in to play that week's criminal suspects, while the director of photography guaranteed the style. At an age when many people relish the idea of retirement, I was still filled with both mental and physical energy, and I finally agreed: if this genre was all that was available, it might be better to try my hand at it rather than being at loose ends.

Fortunately, Paul Alan represented key players at Dick Wolf's production company and was able to persuade them to hire me for an episode of *Law & Order: Special Victim's Unit* that was being produced at Chelsea Pier in Manhattan. This was once again hailed as a big breakthrough. The show was going into its fourth year and had hired only one female director in each of the previous seasons. All had been found "wanting." The same was true of just about every prime-time series, including cable. Tom, like millions of Americans, had loved watching the original *Law & Order* and its many reruns, often late at night, and I used to tease him about it. "You know how it's going to end, why watch it?" "It's like in the Bible" was his semi-serious reply. "Even though you know that Abraham will not kill Isaac the inner story still keeps you in suspense." That sounded smart, but it was not very helpful for what I was about to undertake. Luckily, I was sent copies of past *SVU* episodes to study the style I would soon have to copy.

One aspect of the show did mystify me at first. Each episode had at least one scene in the squad room where the detectives gathered to review evidence, and it was always filmed in one continuously moving shot. It took several viewings to realize the key to the staging: the dialogue was purposely written to be handed off from one detective to the next. If the scene started with Detective A speaking, the camera would dolly with him as he walked towards the coffeepot, passing Detective B seated at her desk who would then speak the second line as she got up, and then dolly with her as she walked towards a blackboard to scribble a clue while passing Detective C seated at his desk who would respond, and so it would go. There were endless variations on the ways to keep this going. In fact, the key rule in all these procedural shows was to keep the camera in motion as much as possible, with the actors walking and talking down corridors, lobbies and Manhattan streets with information always exchanged in hurried tones.

Of course, I was a bit tense when I first arrived, wanting to do well. Usually, a director in episodic TV shows up a week before shooting to cast the secondary players, choose locations and, if lucky, be handed the script before the first day of filming. I arrived two weeks ahead just to observe as much as I could without having any responsibility. It was a very efficiently run factory. As soon as the principal actors and the crew completed one episode, they went on to the next with the new director, without a break until the season ended. My first official day started with a reading aloud of the script, with Ted Kotcheff, the executive producer, taking his seat at the head of the table, with the heads of the various departments seated around him, all befitting a man whose pedigree included the feature *North Dallas Forty*. Ted had the iconic look of a film director: tall and broad-shouldered, and he had a big voice that he was not at all shy to use. I had been part of many table reads and expected that all of us would pitch in and take the roles of the absent cast, so I was taken aback when Kotcheff took every part for himself, leaving little doubt as to who was top dog. "Ah, well," I thought, "I can live with that for a month," and I went off to scout locations, the only permanent sets being the squad room and the morgue, knowing I had to return in the late afternoon to take part in casting the episode's victim of the week, a teenage girl.

Her story, like every other one in the series, involved a sex crime taken from real life, and this one was extremely disturbing; luckily the crime would be described in testimony in the courtroom, and I wouldn't have to film it. A number of fine actresses came in to read for the part, and, at the end of the auditions, I offered my thoughts about the girls we had seen. Ted didn't agree with my choice and picked somebody else, which was fine with me, but, as the gathering broke up and I was heading out the door, he asked me to step into a side office and closed the door. I had no idea what he wanted to tell me in private but wasn't very worried — everything so far had been quite amiable. Without a preamble he launched in. "You might think you're somebody, but around here you're nothing."

My years of directing films where producers and directors had fruitful, sometimes heated, discussions about casting had ill prepared me for that shocking attack. I'd been undermined or insulted before but never in such a ruthless manner. In the first seconds I thought that my crime had been thinking I could offer an opinion but as I wandered back to the stage where they were shooting a scene, I saw Ted warmly chatting away with a male director who regularly worked on the series, his arm draped around the fellow's shoulder. He appeared so at home, so relaxed in every fiber of his body, I instantly knew that for Mr. Kotcheff I was that thing called a female intruder who had been forced on him against his will. That evening, after years of being free of them, I had a full-blown anxiety attack. Fortunately, the friend I was staying with was a doctor and gave me an Ativan pill which helped to calm me down. Like Sydney Pollack, Kotcheff hovered over me for the rest of the episode. If his plan was to undermine confidence in the decisions I made on set, he didn't do a bad job. I was a half-day behind schedule, which is not a good thing if you hope to be asked back.

Unfortunately, I needed to keep working; the income would keep Tom from worrying about his rising medical bills, the worst thing possible for a person fighting for his life. My indefatigable agent went to work once again, and I was more than a little surprised to be hired to direct an episode of yet another Dick Wolf show, *Law & Order: Criminal Intent*, also filming in downtown Manhattan. I knew that all would go well this time around since the producer in charge was my friend Fred Berner, whom I had worked so well with on the Gene Wilder film. Our casting sessions were collegial, and Frank Prinzi, the director of photography, was someone whose work I admired. I had been warned in advance that the lead actor in the series, Vincent D'Onofrio, was often insulting to visiting directors, but everything went surprisingly smoothly. So much so that after the episode aired, I was asked back. I was by now used to dealing with all of Vince's demands, such as exercising for an hour in a gym set up especially for him near the set while he kept the entire crew waiting each morning. He was the irreplaceable star — the series had been built around him, unlike the other *Law & Order* shows — and everyone had to accommodate him, like it or not. I wasn't too surprised when he informed me during a break that he was the best actor living.

Fred and I were set to cast two excellent actors as that week's criminal suspects when we faced an unexpected wrinkle: Vince recommended a student of his for the younger suspect, an actor we had already auditioned and passed on. Wanting to oblige, we had the young man back to read a second time, which confirmed that we had made the right decision and went with our first choice. Little did either of us know what a grudge Vince was carrying until it burst out during filming. We had barely begun rehearsing a scene when our star abruptly turned towards me. "Joyce, we have to talk." I thought to myself, "Oh no, here we go again," sure that he was about to complain about the young actor we had cast in spite of his wishes. With angry steps, he led the way to a corner of the office building we were using as a set. He didn't waste any time before going on the attack. "I have never been so insulted in all my life! How can you cast Terry O'Quinn (the older actor) and expect an actor like *me* to work with him!" And off he stormed. There wasn't even a second to get in a word edgewise, but if there had been, I certainly wouldn't have wasted it defending the highly talented Mr. Quinn, especially knowing how thoroughly Gene Wilder had enjoyed performing with him in our Cash Carter mystery. I feared that the poor fellow would now be paying the price for Vince's misdirected anger. As I stood there, Terry, concerned for me, came over and asked what had happened. "Oh, nothing to worry about. Everything's just fine."

Vince wasted little time calling Dick Wolf's LA office to tell them of my crime, and I knew then that I would never be hired a third time. My pal Fred Berner never spoke up to remind the other executive producers that the final casting decision had been his; his self-protecting silence hurt much more than any actor's stupidity. As I was leaving the set on my last day, the sound recordist came up to tell me that he wished to apologize, on behalf of the crew, for Vincent's behavior. It was a fine thing to say, and it meant a lot to me. Equally appreciated was a going away present I received from Frank Prinzi: a DVD of *The Wanderers*, one of my favorite Philip Kaufman films, with a sound track so wonderful that, whenever I play it, I can't keep myself from dancing.

After that experience and a stint on another NBC crime show with another dominating male producer, it was more than clear that I wasn't cut out for the limited role of the episodic TV director on network television. I would love to have been hired by one of the truly innovative shows going into production at HBO, but there was little hope of my being considered since so many well-known feature directors were eager to work in the once-scorned medium, especially now that the studios were making fewer films, lusting after action blockbusters that played worldwide. While all this was happening, Tom had been in Sloan Kettering's isolation ward, recovering from the stem cell transplant and suffering from all the predicted side effects. Due to my work schedule, I had only been able to visit him late at night while he was sleeping, but at least I was able to be by his side should he wake up.

It had been a harrowing experience. After Tom was admitted to an isolation room at the hospital, I watched as a nurse injected his harvested stem cells back into his bloodstream as she sang, "Happy Birthday, dear Tom," in harmony with the doctors and aides standing at the foot of his bed. With face masked and body gowned like the others, I eagerly joined that white-clad chorus, all of us knowing that the slightest germ could finish Tom off. All seemed well at first, but within hours every system in his body reacted violently, and this continued for days. It was awful to watch, yet he never complained. The body is a miracle; three weeks later it had grown a new immune system on its own, allowing Tom to be discharged cancer-free. Instead of heading for the nearest bed, he insisted on walking one mile along the Hudson River and breathing in the cold winter air, so happy to be seeing another day.

Of course, our hero collapsed after that and limited himself to briefer walks on our Roxbury roads. I was so very glad to be home with him and did all I could to make him comfortable, cooking the food he liked most at the top of my list. I did try having a few friends over for dinner to vary his day but had to give that up since he would quickly fade, often before I served the main dish. What did tempt him out occasionally was going to our local movie theater with Arthur and his new lady friend, Agnes Barley, a painter he had met after Inge Morath, his wife of many years, had died. Agnes was Sarah's age, which I had found shocking when he first brought her to our house but quickly got over it as they seemed to be falling in love. Since the pair always held hands like teenagers when we went out, I always felt like we were double-dating. Agnes was adorable and warmhearted, and Arthur was a very lucky man to have found her.

In spite of my vow to stay away from directing episodic shows, I thought no harm could possibly come to me from directing one in which Treat Williams, with whom I had stayed close over the years, was the star. If it proved to be anything like my experience with Gene Wilder, he would protect me from interfering showrunners. With Tom's blessings and assurances that he would be fine on his own for another month, I flew out to Salt Lake City to begin work with my old friend and the cast of *Everwood,* the show's name coming from the fictional Western town where Treat was playing a widowed doctor trying to raise two kids on his own. I could sense almost immediately that Treat was far from happy the minute I arrived. When the show first aired, the children were secondary characters. Now that they were in their teens and good looking, the story line had shifted to them, with the grownups pushed more and more into the background. But Treat did his job, and the producers were so pleased with my work that I was hired to direct another episode just a few months later. I didn't hesitate, sure that nothing could possibly go wrong this second time around.

The new episode had a subplot that revolved around a budding romance between Treat and his attractive neighbor. As silly as it may sound, trouble began with a scene that found the good doctor kneeling side-by-side with the lovely lady, hosing down her dirty bathtub in which his kids had bathed her flea-ridden dog. The wardrobe assistant had dressed Treat in a long-sleeved shirt and buttoned it up to his neck. I saw him arguing with her and went over; he was by now opening the top buttons and rolling up the sleeves, insisting that it was appropriate to the watery action at hand. He was so obviously right, I readily agreed and was about to call "Action," when the costume supervisor herself stormed on to the set and told me that the unbuttoned shirt was *impermissible* — no strands of chest hair would be allowed to show. Treat, really angry by now, said it was pure ageism; he was sure that if one of the teenage boys showed chest hair it would be acceptable. Caught between the two, I chose what was right for the scene, as is my instinctive habit, but clearly chose wrongly since my agent got an earful about my bad behavior. Instead of bringing up my having sided with Treat, the producer reported that I wouldn't be hired a third time because not one actor wanted to work with me. The charge was so preposterous that I could barely keep myself from howling.

That was almost topped by a call I received from Matt Penn, the executive producer of the original *Law & Order*. I doubt he knew that I was now untouchable in the Dick Wolf realm when he invited me to be part of a small panel of their top directors who would represent all three of their shows at a Director Guild symposium in Manhattan. Its purpose was to introduce aspiring directors to the workings of episodic TV. I thought my participating would be ludicrous and was about to refuse, when my curiosity, once again, won out. I took my place on the stage, seated between Ed Sherrin and Gus Makris who, between them, had directed hundreds of the shows' episodes. We were each introduced with clips from our work and asked to speak before questions were invited from the audience.

Up until the last minute, I had planned to stand up and say, "Ladies and gentleman. You see before you a female director who has been trotted out to show the world that *Law & Order* welcomes women. It's a lie!" But when I looked out at the upturned faces of the young women seated in the many rows, I just couldn't do it; they were all looking up at me with so much hope in their eyes. At least, that's what I thought. What I knew, moments later, was that I had plain chickened out and wasted my chance to strike a blow, however minor, against discrimination. It likely would have caused a minor commotion and been reported in *Variety* and the *Hollywood Reporter*, getting the kind of attention that the women's committee at the Directors Guild has been attempting to achieve for years. A picture of me sitting on stage with fellow (male) directors appeared in the Directors Guild magazine, causing me to feel like a collaborator in a scam, a most disturbing role to have played.

fourteen

ARTHUR MILLER DIED. It was a blow to the theater world, but for Tom, the sudden loss of one of his closest friends was particularly hard. He pulled himself together the day after it occurred to do an interview with Terry Gross for NPR's *Fresh Air,* telling stories that spoke to Arthur's wonderful humor. Alas, the stem cell transplant had given him only one year's remission, and I had been driving him down to Sloan Kettering for infusions of new drugs. He had been writing intermittently, but with each drip of chemo his ability to focus lessened. Thankfully, he was able to derive intense pleasure from clearing a trail, "Tom's Folly," through our woods and taking the children of friends out there for magical mystery tours. He was so very determined to have "more life" that he opted, once again, to check into a Sloan Kettering isolation ward for another stem cell transplant, which he knew from the previous one would make him unbearably sick for weeks. This time it took him even longer to recover from that assault, and the results were disheartening: the remission didn't last for more than six months, and we would be looking for drug trials he might qualify for before the year was over.

Early in the remission, when we still had hopes of it lasting, Paul Alan had called once again with news of a possible job directing a film about an American Girl doll. I thought he was kidding; animation was the last genre I knew anything about. But, no, he was talking about a film *based* on a doll. Our local librarian, Marnie, amused at my ignorance about the American Girl universe, informed me that there was not just one doll, but a series of them from different historical periods — the Revolutionary War, the Depression, World War II, et cetera — accompanied by fictional stories told from the perspective of girls living through those times.

The dolls and books were so popular that Marnie had been hosting monthly tea parties at the library for local girls who brought their dolls and discussed their favorite parts of their now favorite stories. The heroine of the script that I was e-mailed was Molly McIntire, a rambunctious and self-involved ten-year-old whose world changes when her physician father is called up to serve overseas in the middle of World War II. The screenplay greatly appealed to me as I would, once again, have the pleasure of working with girls not much younger than the ones in my documentary *Girls at 12*. Added to that, I could delve into the '40s radio shows — *Jack Benny, The Fred Allen Show* — and pop music that were so much a part of my own childhood and that would now form the background sounds of Molly's life. If I got the job.

Julia Roberts's production company had obtained the movie rights to the stories, but I never got to meet her. Her former agent, now partner, Elaine Goldsmith-Thomas, was the producer in charge. Paul Alan had warned me that Elaine had a reputation as being somewhat of a tyrant, and so I was curious to see what new form of bullying I might encounter when I met her at her New York office. Happily, there was none. I had learned a great deal since my first outing with Sydney Pollack: invite suggestions and, when they are good, be happy, and, if not, pretend they are good while quietly going your own way as much as possible. I thought a little show and tell would aid my audition as directors are absurdly asked about their "vision for the film" even if they received the script just the day before. I took photos of period-perfect streets and houses in a nearby Connecticut town, spread them out on Elaine's desk as examples of what I thought Molly's world would look like. It must have worked; by the time I arrived home I was hired.

To round out my knowledge, I drove back down to Manhattan to see the American Girl store on Fifth Avenue with my own eyes. The scale of it stunned me. It occupied a four-story building on the corner of 49th Street where girls could take their dolls for a shampoo and ask their indulgent parents, or more likely grandparents, to purchase more accessories for them. They could even invite their dolls to a tea party in the top-floor restaurant, where small baby seats were clipped to all the tables. To their credit, they also had rows of books on the first floor that instructed girls in everything from opening a bank account and starting their own business to one about "your changing body," with questions and answers about "bras, periods, pimples, and everything in between." I wish I had been able to get such advice when I was a kid when the euphemism "falling off the roof" was the only way to name our monthly unnamable.

The usual financial reasons took us to the Toronto area, and our location scout found a nearby town, Port Hope, that had a period-perfect Main Street, complete with a restored movie theater where our own film would open with Molly and her two best friends watching *Movietone* newsreels (which preceded most movies in the 1940s) which I had the fun of re-creating by digitally splicing together old newsreel clips. The town even had a period-perfect drugstore with a 1940s soda fountain, complete with red leather swivel stools and bowls for banana splits, where our girls could enjoy their ice cream floats. I had noticed at our first rehearsal that our young actresses slouched in their jeans and suggested that they wear skirts or dresses next time we met, explaining that it would not only be appropriate to the period but it would change the way they held their bodies. It worked; they sat straighter, and it helped them to easily slip into their new roles. It was a happy set, from the talented cast that included Molly Ringwald, who played Molly's mother, to our cameraman, Rodney Charters, who was on a summer break from the hit series *24* with Keifer Sutherland and was able to use his relationship with Panavision to secure their breakthrough Genesis camera before it hit the market. It was the first digital camera to be compatible with 35mm lenses, producing an image quality amazingly like film.

As part of the contract with the American Girl Company, we not only had to dress Molly as she was depicted in the many books about her but also duplicate the exact look of her bedroom, down to the pillows and coverlet on her bed. We wound up building sets for all the interior scenes, taking care that the windows matched the ones in the house we chose for all the exterior scenes. The built sets were a luxury but a very efficient one as they permitted us to remove walls for camera moves, so welcoming after the many TV films I had directed whose limited budgets dictated shooting in real locations. The other practical luxury we had was a "B" or second camera that allowed us to shoot close-ups while the "A" or principal camera was filming wider angles. Although it meant hiring a second operator and assistant, it was worth every penny in time saved.

I got to edit in Manhattan so I could go back to Roxbury to be with Tom on the weekends, and I was pleased with the finished film, which is one of my favorites. The only off note came at the very end when Elaine decided to host a screening in New York with all the young cast flown in for the occasion. Afterwards, when the lights came up, she stepped on to the stage, introduced herself as the producer and invited the cast, one by one, to stand beside her and thanked them for their performance. She even called up her two associate producers for their own round of applause. I patiently waited for my name to be called, assuming I would be last, following the practice of opening film credits. It never happened. My young actresses were puzzled, our editor fumed, but I wasn't much surprised. Producers can rarely keep themselves from taking full credit.

Back home, and anticipating *Molly*'s broadcast, I suddenly felt an overwhelming, almost urgent need to call Jim Glennon. We had rarely spoken since our quarrels over politics, but my deep affection for him had never lessened. He picked up immediately and told me he had just been admitted to Cedar Sinai Hospital but said "No worries, it's nothing serious, just a blood clot in my leg." It seemed that he had been filming on the set of the HBO show *Big Love* and had kept working in spite of tremendous pain. It was the assistant director who forced him to go the hospital. He wasn't surprised that I had called and reminded me that, years ago, I had a nightmare in which he fell off a mountain and phoned to tell him about it, only to learn that he had been thrown from his racing bike on a steep mountain trail just the day before. Now, fighting for breath, he expressed what we both knew to be true but never said aloud. "Joyce, you and

I have always had some unexplainable deep connection." Jim died a week later from complications resulting from prostate cancer. He was sixty-four.

It was as though a vital part of me had been ripped off, a part I had assumed would always be there even when I didn't tend to it. Our quarrels over politics now seemed so stupid. The HBO producers held a memorial service to honor him at the Egyptian Theater in Los Angeles, but I couldn't leave Tom to attend. Laura Dern reported back to me that the place was packed with the crew and casts that had loved him for his humor and eternal optimism as I did, many offering up quotes from his oft-repeated lines on the set, or what I teasingly referred to as *The Sayings of Chairman Jim*. I don't know if he ever said to another director what he often said to me when lining up a shot for me to approve: "Empress, put your festering eye on that socket and take a look." It may not sound like it to other ears, but it was a humorous tribute to the art of collaboration, and I loved him for it.

Tom had a wish — to travel one last time to Italy before he died. Given his poor stamina, we decided to limit ourselves to one week in Rome. Knowing we were tight on funds, his sister Elizabeth recommended we find a place to stay through an unusual travel guide, *Bed & Blessings,* with its list of convents and monasteries that rented rooms to help them stay financially afloat. We found one in an ideal location, just a few blocks from the Spanish Steps and the Trevi Fountain, into whose waters Anita Ekberg had submerged her luscious body in *La Dolce Vita*. In spite of the rock-hard mattresses and the shared bathroom that accounted for the exceptionally low price of the convent room, we loved it and felt like kids sharing an adventure. The nuns were gracious about everything but the curfew. The massive wooden doors were locked at 10PM, which suited us just fine, save for the one night we had to race through the streets like truant schoolchildren, the price for having dined too leisurely in Roman fashion.

Once back home, all our attention turned to the Obama-McCain race that was nearing its nail-biting climax, and it was impossible to think of anything else. When the evening of November 4 finally arrived, we sat together, glued to our TV as the polls closed, barely able to breathe. By 8:15PM we were shouting with joy. Barack Obama had won. Our first thought was, "How we wish Arthur could have lived to see this," remembering the day, eight years before, when the Supreme Court handed the presidency to Bush and Arthur had grimly declared, "It's all over." He had lived through the circus of the McCarthy hearings, refusing to testify against his fellow writers, yet in his mind all that paled next to the permanent damage he predicted the Bush presidency would do to our country. I carefully cut out the color photo of Michelle and Barack from the front page of the *New York Times* as they walked down Pennsylvania Avenue after the inauguration ceremony, Michelle's bright yellow dress and coat symbolizing in my mind our brighter future.

Tom had pushed himself to stay alert until that night. Within a few days, his kidneys began to fail, and we were told that he needed to be hooked up to a dialysis machine twice a week to stay alive. Entering a hospital basement flooded with fluorescent lights and seeing a dozen people in end-of-life condition hooked up to those machines was a frightening sight, and I dreaded leaving Tom alone there, even for a few hours. But, being Tom, he stoically accepted it. I knew it was wishful thinking on my part, but I got busy researching portable dialysis machines, dreaming of keeping him at home comfortably and even travelling now and then; doing the busy work was far easier than acknowledging that his death was near. A month later, actually the day before Christmas, the physician in charge of an experimental drug trial he had qualified for up in Boston gave him the worst news possible: not only had the drug failed to work, he couldn't hold out hope of any other drug slowing the disease either.

The doctor then went on to present to Tom two choices that were unthinkable — live in debilitating pain for perhaps six months or stop dialysis and die within a few weeks, with morphine to ease the way. Sarah had joined us, and the two of us sat in shocked silence with our hands clasped, while Tom seemed to be absorbing the news, but it was hard to tell since his eyes were now closed. After what seemed like an eternity, he quietly said, "I prefer to die now."

There was silence in the car as I drove us back to Roxbury, each of us trying to absorb Tom's decision until Sarah suddenly remembered that it was now Christmas Eve and we had made plans to meet Karen and Gene for dinner at the Mayflower Inn near our home. The thought struck Tom as so absurd that he instantly cheered up and started to sing Christmas carols, with Sarah and me giddily harmonizing along. Gene and Karen must have thought we had already been drinking when we arrived an hour late. No sooner had we sat down, Tom told them about his resolution to end his life, knowing that Gene had survived a stem-cell transplant to rid his body of non-Hodgkin's lymphoma a few years earlier, had cared for Gilda Radner right until her end and had more than enough imagination to fill in the blanks of Tom's terrifying roller-coaster ride. With really nothing left for us to say, we silently raised our glasses high and toasted the brief lives we had been given together on this earth. Then, throwing all dietary restrictions to the wind, Tom ate a juicy steak, followed by a chocolate soufflé washed down by many glasses of red wine.

On Christmas Day morning, Tom woke up, and, as he greeted me, his words made little sense. He was in a very sweet mood but clearly something was wrong. With Sarah's help, I was able to get him dressed and drove to our local hospital, where the doctor on call explained that his kidneys hadn't been able to clear the alcohol from the night before. For the first time since Tom got sick, I was at a complete loss as to what to do next. It felt like everything that I held dear was slipping away very fast. Then, the moment we got back to the car, I suddenly realized that Tom hadn't honored a pact he had made with Dr. Comenzo when he first started treatment at Sloan Kettering seven years earlier: he would only "pack it all in" when the good doctor could look him in the eye and tell him that there was no hope left. That would mean going back on dialysis long enough to clear his head and reach Comenzo to discuss his life-ending decision. With his fever rising, I didn't dare bring him back home and drove straight to a regional hospital where he could receive dialysis and round-the-clock medical care. By then, he didn't know where he was.

He was quite agitated that first night, but I succeeded in getting him peacefully settled with the lights off, opened up my laptop, slid in a disc and snuggled close to watch an old Sid Caesar *Show of Shows,* filled with silly skits that never failed to amuse him. Suddenly, just as he was about to drift into sleep, the door was flung open and I heard a man call out in a jovial voice, "I hear there's a Jew here!" The figure of a man with a large-brimmed black hat and black coat that reached down to his shoes was silhouetted in the doorway. I knew immediately that it was a Hasidic Lubavitcher rabbi. Without waiting for us to invite him in, before I could even get up to stop him from entering the room, the rabbi was at Tom's bedside ready to recite prayers. Tom must have answered "Jewish" when the registration nurse had asked his religion when he was admitted earlier in the evening in a less-than-lucid state. The rabbi was excited because there were so few practicing Jews in the area, and he thought he had at last found one.

I was torn between outrage at the intrusion, ready to toss him out, and mirth at the absurdity of the situation since I knew myself to still feel irrationally under attack at the sight of a rabbi. No wonder, when I remembered that the last time I had been this close to one was the evening we were sitting shiva at my brother's house for my mother who had just died, and the local rabbi had refused to allow mom's much-loved granddaughters, who had both had their bat mitzvahs, be part of the mourner's quorum. But, ever the gentleman, Tom let the rabbi pray over him for a while and finally fell asleep, but not before insisting that I go home to rest.

When I arrived early the next day, Tom was aware that his clarity was rapidly fading; if he was going to speak with Comenzo it had to be right away. I picked up the phone near his bed and offered to help him place a call to Ray, but Tom adamantly refused to take the receiver; talking by phone would not do, they had to be in the same room. It seemed impossible: he was bedridden in a Connecticut hospital, and Ray had just taken a new job as director of the stem cell lab at Tufts Medical Center in downtown Boston, a four-hour drive away. With Tom growing ever more agitated, I was finally able to reach Ray at his home. It was a Saturday, and he kindly offered to meet with Tom first thing Monday morning at his lab.

With the hospital's reluctant blessing and extra blood transfusions to help him survive the journey, Tom and I set out the next afternoon for a motel on the Charles River where we were to spend the night. Early the next morning, a close and constant friend from Cambridge days, Rikk Larsen, was waiting, and I let out a huge sigh when he hugged me. Just getting Tom into his trousers and shirt and then into the wheelchair to the elevator had left me trembling. We were driving across the Longfellow Bridge when I noticed that both the bridge and the Boston streets were strangely empty and belatedly realized that, of course, it was Martin Luther King Day, that Comenzo was generously coming in just to see Tom. The hospital's lobby was as empty of people as the streets, and, without anyone to ask for directions, Rikk and I wandered hopelessly lost in its long corridors. I finally saw Ray in one of them waving at us, his hand already stretched out in greeting. Tom didn't know who he was.

Gesturing to follow him, we found ourselves in a large office flooded with sunlight where Rikk retreated to a corner of the room to give us a sense of privacy. Ray tried once again to engage Tom in conversation, but it seemed hopeless; his eyes were closed, his head was drooping on his chest. To cover the awkwardness and fill the air with noise, I introduced Rikk and told Ray a condensed version of my friend's rather remarkable life story, a part of which involved adopting Vietnamese children just as Saigon was falling. Ray thought the saga fascinating, and at the end he turned to Tom and asked, "How come you never turned this into a movie?" Head still bowed and eyes closed, Tom uttered one word, "Sloth." We were absolutely astonished. Tom's clarity had returned, along with his usual wit. Then, as though this was the beginning of a social visit, Tom asked Ray if he was enjoying his new life in Boston. They chatted easily for a while until, almost casually, as if they were talking about the weather, Tom asked the man who had kept him alive longer than he

could have ever hoped for, "Ray, is it time?" "Yes, it is," Ray softly
answered. We said our last good-byes and drove home.

Tom died quietly in his own bed two weeks later. Hospice nurses
came for a few hours each day to make him comfortable. When he
was coherent enough to talk, he would ask his visiting friends if
they believed in an afterlife and was surprised at how equivocal most
answers were except for that of his tennis buddy, Frank, who was
sure he was going to heaven, or rather his version of one. Tom's
brother, Morrill, arrived with a complete set of Bach recordings and
two speakers, which he hooked up to Tom's computer on a nearby
desk. Tom had told him years before that listening to Bach's preludes
and fugues "ordered his mind," and so they played almost nonstop
until the end. The visit I was most touched by was from a male attendant who groomed him, swaddled him in blankets and wheeled him
outdoors in the February sun to gaze up at the maples and the towering pines. Then, when the nurse told Sarah and me that he would
die within two days at the most, I stopped all activities and barely
left the room; I wanted to be by his side when the end came. I did
step away briefly when a few friends came by, only to be hastily summoned back. Tom had grown agitated, called out for a sip of water,
but when one of them put it to his lips, he pushed it violently away.
"No, no, I want my loved one." I froze in joy hearing those words,
his very last gift to me, knowing that I would never hear them again.

I then did something I'll always regret. I hurried out to pick up a
book in the next room when I heard what sounded like a long sigh
coming from the bedroom, a sound unlike anything I had ever heard.
Calling out to Sarah to come quickly, we both entered the room
cautiously. At first glance, we weren't sure if Tom was still alive and
stood there as still as he was, not daring to breathe. I checked his
pulse; there was none. Still unsure, Sarah found a small mirror and,
with some embarrassment, placed it under his nose just as she had
seen done in the movies. But not a trace of mist was to be seen. All
that remained was this miraculous shell that had contained Tom for
seventy-five years.

Perhaps it would have helped me deal with the grief stored up in me if I had flung myself on his body and wept, but I was too numb and the prearranged ritual of disposing of the dead only reinforced the numbness. The hospice nurse arrived, pronounced Tom officially dead, signed a certificate and handed it to me. Two men from the cremation service entered soon after with a rolling stretcher to remove his body from the bed and zip him into a bag, but it was too painful to watch, and I left the room. They wheeled the stretcher holding Tom's body across the living room where I paced nervously, out the porch door and across the same lawn where this lover of birds had sat gazing happily at bare winter branches just days before. A week later, I received in the US mail a small box containing his ashes in a plastic bag. That was it. With family and a few close friends, we took turns scattering half of them on a snowy hillside that Tom had nurtured to life over the years, uncovering a field of myrtle and golden daffodils that would fill our house each spring. Sarah recited lines from her father's favorite Pushkin poem about a horseback rider sighting baby pines in a grove of ancient trees:

> I hail you, race of youthful newcomers!
> I shall not witness your maturity,
> When you shall have outgrown my ancient friends,
> And with your shoulders hide their very heads
> From passers-by. But let my grandson hear
> Your wordless greeting when, as he returns,
> Content, light-hearted, from a talk with friends,
> He too rides past you in the dark of night,
> And thinks, perhaps, of me.

fifteen

Those first widowed days flew by in a haze of activities: the reading of Tom's will, probate filing, notifying Social Security, notifying the pension department at the Writers Guild, answering condolence letters, writing to his many friends across the country to invite them to a memorial service that we euphemistically worded "a celebration." Since our house wasn't large enough to hold a hundred people, Ellen and Frank McCourt, who lived down the road in a converted barn, offered theirs. Chairs were rented, food and flowers purchased, arrangements made for my godson, David Grausman, to play the piano. The night before, Ellen phoned me from Tahiti where Frank had been scheduled to give a reading and suddenly collapsed. There was no way for them to return in time, but she insisted that I should feel free to use the house.

Fortunately, Sarah was home with me, and with the help of a dear friend, Susan Monserud, everything was readied. Once again, Sarah spoke graciously and very briefly about Tom, then turned the gathering over to friends who read excerpts from some of his e-mails to them that were really essays that ranged from the books he was reading to politics to the personal. Jokes were made about having to answer Tom's e-mails in kind. Laura Dern, who had flown in from Los Angeles with her two young children, reminisced that while playing Connie in *Smooth Talk* she stayed close by his side, amazed that "this fifty-year-old male MIT professor could give me insight into what this teenage girl was going through." By evening everyone took off to continue their lives, including Sarah, who had to get back to her teaching job at Harvard. I became ill and spent much of my first night alone in the house throwing up. Surrounded by Tom's absence in the long days that followed, I busied myself with repair jobs, painting our bedroom, parts of the kitchen, and the wainscoting in the dining room, all in an effort not to feel too much. When spring arrived, I cleared the fallen branches along the edge of the property with Susan and dragged them to the center of the lawn to set them ablaze.

Sadly, I was back in the Roxbury cemetery before summer was over, along with many of our same friends, when Frank McCourt died and Ellen selected a spot right next to Tom's. It was getting to be the local hot spot since Richard Widmark had died and was buried directly behind Arthur and Inge, with Tom's grave just in front. At the gathering afterwards, many speculated about the conversations our dear departed would be enjoying now that they had all of eternity to consider all aspects of our ever-expanding universe. When I had to return to the cemetery not long after with a few men who were helping me place Tom's headstone — a rock from our woods in which a stone worker had carved his name — a new headstone just to the right of Arthur's caught my eye. Beneath the stone, a couple I wasn't familiar with had been buried who clearly had a fine sense of humor. Since Miller had instructed his children to put the word "Writer" below his name in smaller type, the newly deceased took up the practice of identifying their earthly occupations as well. Beneath their names, was just one word they also hoped to be remembered by: "Readers."

Exactly one year from the day of Tom's death, I had an anxiety attack. My doctor said it was right on schedule, that many of his widowed patients had the same experience, and prescribed a low-dose tranquilizer that helped. Sarah was going through a difficult time of her own. Like all the newly minted PhDs teaching in Harvard's History & Literature Concentration, Sarah had fully expected multiple tenure-track opportunities to come her way. But the collapse of the financial markets the year before in 2008 just as she was receiving her doctorate from Columbia had as chilling effect on academia as it had on every business in the country. Luckily, Sarah wasn't panicked yet since she still had three years left on her Harvard contract and could only hope that hiring would soon resume. When the list of job openings came out the following fall, the situation was even more dismal: there were now double the numbers of recent PhDs from schools like Harvard, Stanford and Yale, and they were all applying for the one good job. Most would soon be facing the choice of abandoning the fields they had spent years becoming experts in or continuing on with an uncertain life as adjuncts, piecing together jobs at multiple colleges that offered no health benefits and very little pay. With her future now looking even more uncertain, Sarah realized she had better broaden her skills and added part-time advising at Harvard to her already busy teaching schedule.

Although my anxiety was at bay thanks to the antidepressant, I found myself spending most of my days unable to get out of bed, listening to fantasy novels on my iPod, with a few Trollope novels thrown in for good measure. A few friends suggested I try meeting men on one of the online dating websites, but I balked at the thought. I wasn't lonely. I missed Tom. Then, without meaning to, my friend Susan got me moving again. At dinner one evening, she told me how unsettled she was feeling without a project to engage her abilities, having recently retired as an architect, and tentatively inquired, "Do you think you and I might do a documentary together?" I didn't take her question very seriously, so I jokingly replied, "Sure. But you come up with a subject." It had been thirty years since I had produced the film about the choreographer Martha Clarke, and making another documentary was the last thing on my mind now, especially as it seemed like I would be going backwards.

But the next day Susan was at my doorstep. "I have a subject." And she began to tell me about a place run by a nonprofit in Lower Manhattan, Gramercy Residence, that was providing a safe home for gay teenage boys who had suffered violence both at home and on the streets and even harder times bouncing from one placement to another in the foster care system. I tried putting her off as indirectly as possible so as not to hurt her feelings. "It's a wonderful idea, Susan, but I can't imagine myself filming there. I have no common ground with those kids." Undeterred, my friend pushed on. "Would you at least visit the place with me? The director is a friend, and I'll take you out for a great lunch afterwards."

Within minutes of entering the old brownstone on East 22nd Street and seeing the kids' wonderful faces I was won over and immediately wanted to be of help, either by volunteering or making the film Susan was pushing for. But where to find the funding? All my old contacts at WNET were long gone, HBO wasn't interested (I was told they had already produced their one film on "that subject") and applying for foundation grants would be a slow process. We felt some urgency to begin; Gramercy's director, Gary Mallon, had mentioned that a volunteer from an acting company was going to help the kids put on a production of Shakespeare's comedy As You Like It, giving us a ready-made structure for the film: the ones who acted in the play would be our main subjects, following their everyday lives in parallel with the rehearsals, all culminating in an opening night performance. Fortunately, when we wrote to friends about the residence and our movie ideas, many pitched in with small donations, allowing us to make a quick start. But that infamous shoe was quietly waiting in the wings to drop; only a few kids showed up at the first rehearsal, and the volunteer left in frustration, giving us our first taste of what it was like to count on traumatized young people to stick to a plan. I was tempted to throw up my hands and walk away; it would be embarrassing, but we could return the donations to our friends.

Without that unifying theatrical production, we were on shaky ground, and the only way I could now think of proceeding was to fully embrace my tried-and-true model; follow three or four of the Gramercy residents and hope a semblance of a story would emerge. But how to pick our subjects? Noticing that most of the residents drifted in and out of the living room, we spent the rest of the week hanging out there, waiting to see if any were curious enough to come over to ask what we were doing. The plan finally worked, especially after six-foot-tall Jasmine discovered we were there to make a movie and offered to become our first subject. Once that happened, the rest followed, and the pain-filled stories we heard were more than enough to comprise a miniseries. Jasmine had arrived as a painfully shy boy named Curtis, having been kicked out of a foster family's home, a family she had come to love, for acting "too gay" and, in less than six months in the more accepting environment of Gramercy, had blossomed socially, made all the more remarkable as she was beginning to transition from male to female.

Dorell, an angry but lovable teenager, had been sexually abused by his older cousin when he was still a baby, then separated from his twin brother and his alcoholic mother by Alabama social services, sthen pent the next fifteen years being transferred, like a package, from one abusive foster home to another, while his more fortunate twin was adopted by a well-off family. Their story was so unusual that I was tempted to make a film just about the twins. Our third subject was Carlos, a poet who had managed to avoid school for most of his eighteen years. His father had disappeared soon after he was born; his mother, Lisette, struggled with substance abuse and had sex for cash in their apartment up in the Bronx. Social workers had removed him from the home when he was ten, but he longed to be reunited with her ever after.

On days we weren't filming, I tried my best to help out by taking Lisette to a nearby community health clinic, but she never followed through on her own; she had as little habit of taking medicine as did Carlos of studying. Although the Gramercy Residence had a certified classroom in the building, neither Carlos nor Dorell completed their GED exams by the time they aged out of foster care the day they turned twenty-one and, by law, were escorted out to the street where the odds would be overwhelmingly against them; half the kids who passed through Gramercy would end up homeless, with, at best, a friend's couch to crash on. Their crime: born poor and gay without a stable family to care for them. Jasmine disappeared, with no known forwarding address.

What followed for the next few years was a sort of dance with my young friends whom I had come to care deeply about. I would research places where they could enroll for free classes at community colleges or tell them about nonprofits that offered job training, but they always had some reason for not keeping their appointments. There were many late-night phone calls asking me for small amounts of cash because they were hungry or needed subway fare for a job interview. It was impossible for me to refuse, even though Susan said I was enabling them. How could I turn my back when Carlos told me that he and his mother, along with what little furniture they owned, were put out on the street because she'd been caught illegally renting out their second bedroom in a government-sponsored apartment for a little extra cash to buy food? After a short stay in a shelter, Carlos found his own solution. He married a man who would support him. As for Dorell, I finally blew up at him after one too many Western Union money transfers and told him never to call me again unless he was employed or at school. To my immense relief, he finally kept his word a few years later and accomplished both.

The film still hasn't been shown on television, but after being a finalist for the PBS series, *Independent Lens*, Susan and I did get a small grant that paid for two thousand DVD copies of the film so that Lambda Legal could donate *Gramercy Stories* to community groups and child welfare agencies across the country, the very places that were supposed to be their protectors.

Having pushed myself to travel into worlds beyond those I had ever known and feeling more than alive again, I was eager to make another documentary. If not for a tall garden weed growing outside my front door, I would have been on my way to Jordan to produce a film about a devout Muslim girl who was about to be the first female in her village to receive a college education. I had been introduced to the subject by Holly Carter, a former *New York Times* journalist who had started a nonprofit, BYkids, partially funded by the Ford Foundation, with a mission to place digital movie cameras into the hands of kids who could tell stories powerful enough to resonate around the globe. Holly was charming and had a knack for recruiting experienced filmmakers to assume the mentorship roles, and I was primed to be seduced. BYkids had already made two award-winning films, one about a 16-year-old AIDS orphan in Mozambique who was creating a new kind of family with other AIDS orphans in his village, and *My Country Is Tibet*, by the sixteen-year-old exiled King of Tibet about his life in Dharamsala as he fought against the obliteration of his people's identity.

One evening, needing a break from reading about the dismal progress of women's education in the Middle East, I stepped out my front door on the way to my first summer party and caught sight of that lone weed shooting up in a patch of grass I had been carefully nursing back to life. By habit, and without considering that the soles of my shoes were slippery or that the grass might be damp at dusk, I crouched to pull it out and in an instant was sliding backwards so rapidly that I tumbled high in the air over a stone wall and landed flat on my back in the dirt road four feet below. I lay there dazed, not daring to move, all the while cursing myself for my carelessness, while hoping for a car to pass by. After waiting in vain for about a half-hour, I gingerly moved my limbs and, not feeling any broken bones, crawled back up the stone steps, hobbled into the hallway and collapsed on the bed, thinking I had escaped the worst.

As it turned out, my self-diagnosis was dead wrong; I had fractured three vertebrae. Not a good thing to happen at any age but dangerous for a woman about to turn seventy-four whose bones were already thinning. It wasn't just the physical damage that was a blow; it was the realization that I would not be flying to Jordan anytime soon. To my immense relief, Holly was happy to wait out my recovery, and I decided to use the extra time to find out as much as possible about Salma, the young girl I would soon be mentoring. Holly had been in touch with her through an intermediary and knew where she lived, how many brothers and sisters she had, the name of the college she would be attending. But she was scant on the kind of more personal information that would give me a sense of who the girl was before I actually put a camera in her hands. When I learned that she could be reached by phone, I devoted some serious time leafing through a tourist guidebook, hoping to learn a few phrases in Arabic, all the while praying the girl could speak a bit of English.

I shouldn't have worried. Salma answered my call in fluent English. "This is amazing and will definitely make my job far easier," was my first thought. She was bubbling over with excitement about her older sister's upcoming wedding, glad that I would be delayed by three months so she could film the traditional ceremony, a culturally rich moment and a seamless way to meet the whole extended family. I was already picturing the music and the dancing intercut with Salma talking with her older aunties about their own girlhoods at a time when hopes for even a third-grade education seemed laughable. My mind couldn't help but turn to her sister. "Is the bride very sad about not attending college like you?" "Oh, she already has her PhD. All my sisters do." To say I was dumbfounded when she casually tossed off this bit of extra information is putting it mildly; any of her uneducated aunts would have been a more suitable subject. Clearly, there had been a terrible mistake; the wrong girl had been selected and Holly would have to apologize for stirring up her hopes.

The hardest part of my recovery was weaning myself from the oxycodone that had been prescribed to ease my severe back pain. It took a month of misery, but I managed and towards the end was ready to get moving again. When I looked over Holly's list of possible subjects, nothing seemed quite right. Then I remembered that my friend Kathy Sreedhar ran a nonprofit that worked to change the lives of marginalized people in India. When I reached Kathy in D.C., she was a gold mine of ideas, and once she understood I was looking for stories about kids, she told me about a residential school for tribal girls three hours north of Mumbai. "The Untouchables?" "No, the *Tribals*. They are people outside of the caste system. There are about ninety million of them in India. Didn't you know that?"

Embarrassed to admit that I had never heard of a population called the Tribals, I turned to my computer where I learned they are the original inhabitants of India, that their land had been stolen from them centuries ago and that they continued to live in extreme poverty. Many still worked as slaves to landlords because they couldn't repay the small loans that had been passed down to them from fathers and grandfathers, despite the fact that this form of bondage had been illegal since 1947, when India achieved its independence from Britain.

But I did learn more hopeful news. In the 1990s, with the help of Vivek Pandit, a Brahman who took up their cause, a dozen Tribal men and women found the courage to defy their owners and "walked off the job." Today the union they formed has over 80,000 members and is growing. Wanting to help the most vulnerable among them, they had built a residential school for their daughters who would become the first females in their villages to receive an education.

It was a great story, and when I relayed it to Holly she was as excited as I was. With permission from Vivek to film, I was put in touch with an adviser who worked at the school, Hindavi Karve, and asked for her help in choosing a girl to mentor — ideally someone imaginative, smart and strong enough to carry a camera. She sent me, via e-mail, case studies of six girls among the two hundred studying there. One sixteen-year-old stood out: Jayshree Janu Karpede, who had written what her mother's response had been when, at the age of ten, she begged to be sent to school. "Education is one of the luxurious things we poor people cannot afford. So stop thinking about school and pay proper attention towards your siblings and help us to earn our living."

What drew me to the girl was not just that Hindavi labeled her "the most brilliant girl in the school" but also her ability to step outside herself and see her own life as an ongoing story. It was unusual, especially in one so young. When I wrote back to thank Hindavi for her report, I asked if she could make sure that Jayshree's family would agree to have to have their daughter featured in a movie. With permission granted, I was composing a letter to introduce myself to Jayhsree when an e-mail from Hindavi overlapped in my in-box with news that the young girl's mother had just committed suicide, leaving behind two little boys and a six-month-old baby girl. No explanation was offered. It was a shock, and I felt terrible for the young mother I had never met and sure that Jayshree would have to leave school. Instead, Hindavi sent the most remarkable e-mail a week later; Jayshree had returned after four days at home.

"Jayshree and other girls who will be the part of movie was sharing with me that they would like to showcase their struggle in this movie, like how they were working as laborer or care taker of their siblings without attending school, how their parents were opposing them to get enroll in school, then how they came in this school, still how their parents are struggling for their basic needs and hoping that one day their daughter will change their destiny with the power of education and wisdom. Jayshree would like to showcase her recent shattered experience in this movie. Her relatives were forcing her to left the school to look after her younger siblings as they are too young but her father stood strongly at her side and refused this decision of their relatives."

I choked up reading the letter and couldn't help but marvel at how fortunate I was that I would soon be meeting such amazing girls. My young assistant, Catherine (or "Cat"), felt exactly the same way. After a chaotic departure from JFK — our bags filled with equipment were overweight and we had to rush to purchase extra ones — Jayshree was there to greet us with her big smile when we landed in Mumbai, and she was everything I had hoped for in an apprentice filmmaker — shiny-eyed and eager to learn. It was impossible to tell that she had so recently lost her mother. Hindavi took charge and led us through the jammed airport to a waiting driver who settled us into his car for the long journey north of the city, ready to do battle with motorized rickshaws, brilliantly painted trucks and slow-moving cows, all competing for that extra inch of space on the roads.

The walls of the school buildings were practically shaking from schoolgirl energy when we arrived. Many of the girls were as young as five and they seemed to occupy every corner of the scrubby land the Tribals had won back from the state. As Miss Hannigan memorably lamented in the musical *Annie*, "Little girls, little girls, everywhere I look I can see them," but for me the girls were a constant joy. I started mentoring Jayshree by giving her my still camera for a few days to play around with and was astonished by her ability to compose a storytelling frame without a word of advice. She was clearly born to make movies and ready to turn the digital camera on the people and places that showed her life, from a brick kiln site where her aunt and uncle labored away and where she demonstrated how she often carried piles of bricks on her head before she was finally free to attend school, to a union members' trip to inspect a state-run boarding school for less fortunate Tribal girls where there were no books, indoor plumbing or mattresses to sleep on.

Through all of this, Jayshree rarely spoke about her mother's death, and I didn't feel it was right to ask. Then, late one afternoon when her classes were finished, Jayshree told me that she wanted to do an interview with herself and a female dorm attendant that she was close to, not telling me what it would be about. After she had set up her camera in a secluded spot, Jayshree began to tell how the woman had taken her out of class one afternoon, informing her she had been summoned home for a surprise party. When she got there, instead of festivities, she found her mother lying on her bed, dead. At this point, Jayshree began to sob uncontrollably and flung herself in the woman's arms, unable to go on. I was dumbfounded. I could understand the woman's reluctance to tell Jayshree the real reason that she was suddenly wanted home, but to say there was a party? I never found out what had caused the suicide and we decided not to use any of that footage in the film. It was too private.

When the film was finished, Jayshree titled it *Fire in Our Hearts*, words taken from a song the schoolgirls sang with pride each morning in Marati, their language, surrounded by huge posters of freedom fighters including Gandhi and Martin Luther King Jr. Here it is in translation:

> For too long we have been under attack,
> we have been assaulted by injustice.
> But now there is a fire in our hearts,
> we will fight for change.
> For too long we have tolerated our suffering,
> we have watched each other dying at work
> in other people's fields.
> But now we are listening to our hunger,
> we will change our lives.
> Long live our struggle!

When they shouted that last line, *Zindabad!*, with raised little fists, I wanted to join in every time. I knew the girls were receiving a daily dose of indoctrination, but the words were so filled with hope I would gladly hear it sung just about everywhere.

On one of our last evenings, Cat and I were enjoying a leisurely walk back to the motel structure where the school's guests were housed. As we reached our neighboring doors, I suddenly didn't know which one I should enter. My mind was a complete blank, with no memory of how I got there or who I was. Cat thought I was joking at first when I looked around and asked, "Where am I?" then realized I truly didn't know. With my panic now engulfing her as well, Cat managed to guide me to one of the twin beds in my room and cover me from head to toe with quilts to stop my shaking as I kept pleading with her, "Tell me my story, please tell me my story." I simply couldn't remember what she had told me about who I was just seconds before.

Poor Cat was with her considerably older boss in the middle of the night in the middle of a foreign continent without a 911 to call for help; all she could think to do was encourage me to take deep breaths to control my terror. This alarming state continued for about five hours when, a little past midnight, my self suddenly returned, except that I couldn't remember a single thing from the hours prior to our arrival at the motel door. The last memory I had retained was of unfriendly looking people, many of them young, scattered in rows and staring at me. At first I thought it was from a bad dream, but then I was able to remember that I had done an interview, via Skype, right before dinner for a professor job at Syracuse University, something that their film department had invited me to do.

Since the time difference was now favorable to contacting Sarah, I sent her a description of what had just happened and asked if she could figure out what it might be while jokingly lamenting that I would never know how the job interview had gone. After a quick search, she was able to identify my strange experience as "transient global amnesia" and forwarded me an e-mail I had no memory of sending her. "Dearest Sarah Rosie, I did the Syracuse interview and hated it! I was facing a roomful of teachers and students and the questions were along the line of, 'Where do you think the industry is heading?' or 'How will you help me find work in Hollywood?' Not a single question about what I could teach them about making a film. I hope they don't offer me the job!" Thankfully, they never did.

When it was time to pack up and leave, I wished that I could take Jayshree with me for a visit, but it was impossible to get a US visa for an unmarried girl. Vivek arranged a screening of the film, with Jayshree in attendance, for the governor of Maharashtra State, with the hope of influencing policy. It's impossible to know if the film had any concrete effect, but every major newspaper across India picked up the story and interviewed Jayshree. With her poise and charisma, one couldn't help feeling that she was on her way to becoming a political leader someday. Then, a few days after the film aired on PBS, I received a crushing e-mail telling me that Jayshree's father had remarried and requested that she return home; his new wife did not want to care for the former wife's children. Vivek drove hours to her village to try to persuade her to return to the school, but Jayshree couldn't bring herself to abandon her young siblings. I had no way of contacting her, and, even if I could have, we didn't speak each other's language. In person, even without Hindavi to translate, we understood each other perfectly, and it still breaks my heart to think of this vibrant young woman repeating her mother's restricted life. I can only hope that she is finding her way.

sixteen

S ARAH WAS FACING a difficult situation; her teaching contract at Harvard was set to expire, and, without a new position,
she had little choice but to return to Roxbury to live with me. This
was not a happy prospect for her, but she was doing her best to be
cheerful about her entering the world of the unemployed. She had
recently ended a long-term relationship with another English professor, and, to top it all off, she was experiencing health problems
once again, particularly autonomic problems that led to severe diz-
ziness when standing and walking. All of this grieved me greatly as
it would have been a pleasure to have her home with me but not
under these circumstances. I drove up to Sarah's apartment just a
few days before her job was up, arms loaded with empty cartons to
help her pack. The day we were set to drive away, she kept an early
morning appointment with a doctor who would be performing a test
that required her to be put to sleep and, as required by law, signed a
document agreeing to not make any important decisions for the next
twenty-four hours.

It would be a promise impossible to keep. When she arrived back
at her apartment and checked her e-mail, she was astonished to see
a letter from the University of Virginia, a dream job that she had
applied for months earlier and given up on — dean of their Honors
Program as well as a teaching position in the English Department —
was suddenly available. If she was still interested, could she fly down
to Charlottesville for an interview immediately? We stared at each
other, grinning like idiots. A deus ex machina had dropped out of
the Cambridge sky into her living room. But there was a problem.
She would likely come close to fainting when walking to interviews
on the large campus to meet with various committees; until now, she

had managed to hide her health challenges by allowing herself extra time to sit and recover in private. After a restless night, she found the courage to write back to the head of the search committee and told him that she would need disability accommodations. He couldn't have been more welcoming. With bolstered spirits, Sarah hopped on her recently purchased mobility scooter and drew admiring glances as, with hair flying, she scooted fast through Logan Airport with me doing my best to keep up as I accompanied her to the gate.

The campus visit was a success; Sarah liked the people she met, and they must have liked her since she was asked to begin work in just two weeks. Luckily, she was already packed up. The movers were instructed to ship her books and furniture to a Charlottesville apartment not too distant from campus, and it was all done so rapidly there was little time to reflect. Once Sarah was settled in, I drove back to Roxbury in a daze, happy for her and saddened that I would be seeing her less often now that she was a seven-hour drive away. Back home, without a project in front of me, I felt a bit lost. And without Tom and his deep pleasure in nature, the joy I had felt in planting flowers seemed to be gone as well, so much of my own delight having lain in his.

My limbo state continued for many months, with occasional drives to visit Sarah in Charlottesville, made easier by listening to books on tape. With Sarah busy at work, I spent my days walking around Charlottesville, which I knew very little about other than that it was a blue dot in a sea of red. On my first walk in the old downtown, I was taken aback when I wandered into a small park, at the center of which stood a bronze statue of General Robert E. Lee sitting majestically astride his horse, Traveller. It had been unveiled in 1924, and, according to an inscription below, thousands of cheering sons and daughters of the old Confederacy had been on hand to celebrate, including the president of the university where Sarah was now teaching, who gave the dedication speech. A few streets down, I stood before another equestrian statue, this one of Stonewall Jackson, opposite the courthouse. I suddenly remembered that Prince George County in Virginia was famous for closing its public schools for five years rather than integrate them after the Supreme Court ruled that segregation was unconstitutional. Disheartened that this was the city my daughter had moved to, I walked away, and drove back north.

Wanting to tell Gene Wilder about my trip south, I was so happy when he phoned the day I arrived home. No longer finding acting roles that challenged him, and inspired by Chekhov short stories, he had turned to writing romances set in Europe during the World Wars. I became one of his first readers, with chapters frequently arriving by e-mail; my returning comments were largely minor ones, more encouragement than anything else. I enjoyed teasing him that each story had scenes in restaurants where his characters would always order his favorite bottle of Sancerre and that future PhDs would ponder the wine's deep significance. By now, St. Martin's Press had published four of them, the last, *Something to Remember You By: A Perilous Romance,* dedicated to "my friend Tom Cole," with the main character, a cello-playing spy in Nazi Germany, bearing Tom's name. But that day, Gene's phone call was not about his fiction but about the difficulty he was having with walking, something about a brain scan and other tests. The call was unnerving; it was hard to understand him, his story made little sense to me and when we hung up I promised to call him soon.

Through all of this, my friends were sure that I would be moving to Charlottesville soon, but I protested that I couldn't imagine selling my wonderful house and leaving them behind. But on each visit to Sarah, I would drive around different neighborhoods, trying to imagine myself walking those streets. I simply couldn't decide. It was far easier to be distracted by binge-watching episodes of *Downton Abbey,* especially loving Maggie Smith's performance as the Dowager Countess. One of the many subplots involved a character played by her cousin, Isobel Crawley, and her exasperating refusal to accept a handsome duke's repeated marriage offers until, one fine day, she did an about face and decided to marry the handsome duke after all. "And why *now?*" the countess inquired in her snippiest tone. The simple answer: "I know you'll think me foolish, but it's my last chance for a new adventure before I'm done." As they say, lightning struck. If she could make a big change in her life, so could I.

I left for Charlottesville the next day and started searching for a place to live, doing my best to resist the charm of various small country houses not far from the city. I had to remind myself that I would be living alone and didn't need the hassle of another roof repair. Luckily, an apartment in a building on the edge of town, with a balcony and views of the Blue Ridge Mountains, was up for sale, and I grabbed it, knowing that my neighbors were eager to purchase my Roxbury house for the exact price of the place I would be buying. It proved to be easier than I thought to let go of a dwelling that I had loved so dearly, finally seeing Tom and myself as just temporary caretakers of a small part of this beautiful earth.

It was very strange to be moving into a home without Tom. Perhaps for the first time I felt truly alone, with no one to quibble with over where to place the piano or the couch. With most of our old furniture fitting in nicely, the apartment had the look of what I had left behind but only the look since Tom wasn't there. We had collected so many books over the years that I'd had a difficult time choosing which ones to give away to the Roxbury library. I'd also had a problem when I emptied the writing shack and opened the cartons Tom had stashed in every corner. He had saved every letter written to him, going way back to one from his mother consoling him when he was away from home for the first time. Her penmanship put my own to shame.

A happy surprise was a letter dated June 26, 1967, from Martin Segal, the founding president of the Film Society of Lincoln Center, and at the time Samuel Beckett's agent, thanking Tom for dinner and letting him know that he had sent "Sam" his recently published book and that, in return, Beckett had inscribed a copy of *Happy Days* to Tom, which was enclosed. I rushed to the bookcase, and there it was, stashed on a lower shelf. I think Tom had completely forgotten about it. It took me days to sort through the rest of the voluminous correspondence that often made me sad, evidence of how people had taken the time to communicate what they were thinking and feeling in letters before the internet changed it all.

One file in particular filled me with sorrow. It contained a half-finished book that Tom had been unable to continue writing once his brain became too foggy for him to think clearly. It lay there on his desk, tormenting him, as he knew that it was his best work. As I read through the manuscript, I fell in love with Tom's writing once again, with Tom again, and made a vow that, once settled in Charlottesville, I would use every skill I had as an editor to cut the pages down to essay length and try to get it published in a literary magazine, something I was able to do a year later in the *Gettysburg Review,* making me feel that Tom was once again by my side.

But I was so busy unpacking and setting up the apartment for the first months that I barely had time to look at the pages or even notice that Sarah and just a few of her colleagues were the only people I knew in my new hometown. I found a listing of classes taught by retired professors and amateur scholars and was considering either a course on Robert Lowell's poetry or fly-fishing when Holly Carter called with an urgent request: please drop everything and fly down to Nicaragua to produce another film for BYkids. Before I could even say, "Sorry, Holly my friend, but I'm barely settled and I don't—" she informed me that the subject was climate change and the devastating effect it was having on the country. A combination of erratic rainfall and higher temperatures was allowing a fungus to destroy the country's coffee plantations, with harvests reduced by more than 50 percent in the preceding three years alone, impoverishing the already struggling farmers. It was crucial that I make a first trip now to find the young person that I would mentor so that when harvest time came in just a few weeks we would be ready to film. It was a tall order.

Like many people, I was concerned about the future of our planet but, other than donating money, I had never actively joined any initiative to do something about it. Here was my chance, and I took it, hoping that if enough people saw the film it might spur them into real action. Kevin Marinacci, the director of a nonprofit that had been working for decades to aid children in Nicaragua, was contacted by Sammy Chadwick, a BYkids activist, and he generously offered to help us find a teenager whose parents owned a small coffee *finca* and who, like Jayshree, would have the ability to choose key moments from their life that, in this case, showed climate change in action.

With Kevin at the wheel the day after Sammy and I flew to Managua, we headed north to San Juan de Cusmapa, smack in the middle of the region that grows some of the finest coffee beans in the world thanks to its rich volcanic soil. Kevin had come up with a simple plan to save time. Rather than drive randomly around the mountainous countryside, hoping to find the right person, we would head straight to the area's independent coffee growers' co-op. In spite of the late hour — the drive had taken most of the day — the folks who managed the operation were still at work and greeted Kevin warmly, having known him for years. Quickly grasping what we were looking for, they volunteered to look through their register to see which members had teenage children, promising to e-mail a list by morning.

We woke to the beauty of the mountains. With the names of more than a dozen families in hand, we trekked down steep trails to the farmers' small dwellings built into the hillsides where we were graciously invited to take seats on their porch, have a soda and listen while Kevin did most the talking. After three long days, the best candidate to emerge was a spirited thirteen-year-old girl named Edelsin Linette Mendez. Her parents owned a six-acre coffee plantation that, at the best of times, barely kept them going.

When Edelsin offered to show us around the property, I thought I had stepped back into a fabled past — piles of leather reins and saddles, farming equipment I'd seen in old movies — but I was quickly jolted out of my reverie when Edelsin asked me how much money we would be paying her family. "None, really. You'll be helping to make the world aware of the crisis here." Edelsin nodded her head in seeming assent, but I was more than a little unsettled by the exchange. Her question brought to the fore what was painfully obvious: the Mendez family was desperately poor, and Sammy and I, in comparison, were very rich. To add to my disquiet, when we rejoined her parents, Señor Mendez led us on a trail to see for ourselves the row upon row of bare-branched coffee plants, their yellowed leaves curling up on the ground beneath them. It was one thing to read about *roya*, the fungus that was killing the plants, but to actually see the damage it caused was truly awful. As we made our farewells with a promise to be back at the end of the month with our cameras, my heart was full.

As soon as I was back in Virginia I called Gene, eager to see how he was doing. Karen answered. After our usual hellos, she took a breath. "Before you speak to Gene, I want you to know that he has just been diagnosed with Alzheimer's, so use simple words and stick to subjects he already knows." I couldn't believe this was happening, but, as Gene and I spoke, I realized that it was all too true, and an inconsolable sadness rose up in me with every word he uttered. I finally understood why our last conversation had made so little sense.

In a somber mood, I flew back down to Nicaragua, this time with Cat, the assistant who had been with me in India. Cat and I had become close friends, and having her with me on this next venture was going to be more than helpful. In addition to being young and strong and a pleasure to be around, she spoke fluent Spanish, which made teaching our young filmmaker how to be comfortable with a camera far easier. Edelsin immediately took to it and started rather ambitiously to record all the steps involved in harvesting. All the family worked together as a team — parents, children and grandchildren — to pick the ripened coffee cherries spared by the blight. When it got too hot to continue for the day, Señor Mendez used a hand-cranked grinder, the same one his father, grandfather and great grandfather had used before him, to separate the bright red shells from the black beans inside, then pour the treasured "gold" into large sacks. When his horse was loaded up, he led it down the mountain to the coffee co-op in town. If you were to see only the video Edelsin shot of her papa against this vast landscape you would think he lived in paradise.

The members of the co-op were grim but determined men as they spoke of the disaster that had befallen them. "Everything is now out of control, it never rains when it is supposed to . . . It rains very hard in one cycle, and then it doesn't rain again . . . For the infestation, there are no borderlines, no borderlines for the neighboring farms, and that's why we spread it to other countries as well . . . If we stop cultivating coffee because of *roya*, we won't be able to leave our children a better future . . . then we . . . disappear . . . " A local musician put his own sobering words to a folk melody at a saint's day festival that was meant to be a day of celebration and joy:

> I am looking for answers as to why it won't rain,
> My poor little Juan won't get to see the deer,
> My poor little Juan won't get to see the rabbits.
> And if we continue like this,
> Death will be sure for all of us.

We were tempted to end the film with this song but settled instead on hope — shots of Edelsin back in school as she narrates, "I think it will be up to millions of kids like us to stop the disaster." The film aired on PBS, and I can only hope that some of the climate change deniers saw it and were swayed.

My eightieth birthday arrived on schedule, and Susan and Ellen McCourt drove down to Charlottesville to celebrate my having achieved such a majestic age. Settling in with them on my old couches in my new living room healed the distance of my two worlds. As we talked, I couldn't help but recall my teenage horror at the thought of turning sixty (which seemed beyond ancient) and my mother telling me, "You should be so lucky to live that long." But after some more banter, I had to admit that my lack of stamina hiking up and down those mountain trails in Nicaragua had been troubling me, especially as I hoped to continue making movies. Then when I saw Ruth Bader Ginsberg doing pushups with her trainer in the documentary that bears her initials, I was so inspired that the first thing I did when I got home was to Google "Trainers near me." I found a small gym I liked and began going three times a week for the first time in my life. I'm still terrible at those pushups, but there's always hope that I'll be able to do one by the time I'm ninety.

Wouldn't it be wonderful if I could use the strength I'm gaining from those workouts to swoop down into Hollywood just like my childhood heroine, Wonder Woman, and smash open all the barriers that have kept women directors out for all these many years? I've always longed for those bracelets of steel to ward off all and any foes. The Directors Guild magazine that shows up in my mailbox each month only acts as a fuel to set my long-burning anger aflame as I can't resist flipping to the magazine's center pages to read about the feature films that are about to be released. Rarely has there been a female director's face among them. One would think that I would be at peace with the status quo by now, but how can I?

Happily, the pace of change has been picking up in the last few years. Women directors achieved historic highs in 2020 according to the USC Annenberg Inclusion Initiative, with women comprising 15 percent of the filmmakers calling the shots, a major uptick from 4 percent in 2018, capped off by back-to-back Best Director wins at the Academy Awards for Chloé Zhao for her feature *Nomadland* and Jane Campion for *The Power of the Dog*. Although Sian Heder didn't capture that prize, her film *Coda* took the Best Picture award, a truly thrilling outcome for women directors everywhere. The really big change has been in episodic television, with women now directing one-third of those shows, more than triple from ten years ago. It's remarkable when you consider there were hardly any when I was hired to direct *Law & Order SVU* in 2002 and the price of entry was verbal abuse from a producer who didn't want any females around. Even HBO's blockbuster series *Game of Thrones* only hired one woman to direct during its entire eight-season run.

When I think about the #MeToo movement that has finally drawn much-needed attention to sexual abuse of women in the workplace, I find it extraordinary that it all started with an exposé of Harvey Weinstein, one of the men who caused me much pain. Although I had to endure his insults and ceaseless bullying in an editing room, it can't compare to the trauma of the aspiring actresses he lured to his hotel suites and sexually assaulted. Weinstein's trial and the once unthinkable firing of other serial predators like the CEO of Fox Television, Roger Ailes, couldn't help but bring up old memories of how demeaned I felt when I was a young hopeful in Paris and producers touched my breasts. It was considered annoying but normal, something I had to simply accept as a woman if I wanted to work in that all-male world.

I'm also more than gratified that the #MeToo movement has raised awareness about the whole issue of gender inequity in the film business. In an effort to even the odds, the Sundance Film Festival announced in 2019 that, for the first time, they aimed to show an equal number of films by women and men at the festival's upcoming 35th anniversary. The *Hollywood Reporter* pounced on the story and invited me and the six other women who had won the Grand Jury Prize for Best Dramatic Feature in prior years to New York to have a group picture taken. I almost didn't go since it was winter and there was the possibility of falling snow. My flight was only slightly delayed, but by the time I arrived at the Manhattan studio all the other prizewinners were already there, with hair and make-up artists fussing over them. No sooner had I entered than Debra Granik, whose film *Winter's Bone* I greatly admired and whom I had never met, rushed over to greet me. "Oh, I'm so glad you've come. I can't tell you how important your winning at Sundance was to me." Then a few others joined in, voicing the same thought. Apparently I had shown them that it could be done.

POSTSCRIPT

I T'S SARAH WHO is actually responsible for my writing this book. After I finished a third BYkids film about an inspiring teen with cerebral palsy, she warned: "I know you're going to get depressed without a new project, so why don't you write a memoir?" My first reaction was much like the time a friend suggested I do a documentary about having a baby. "That is the most narcissistic . . ." But with little else to occupy my imagination, I typed in a few sentences and just kept going. And maybe that's the point of all this: just keep going.